TOP **10**
COPENHAGEN

ANTONIA CUNNINGHAM

D0230622

DK

EYEWITNESS TRAVEL

Left **Amalienborg Slotsplads** Right **Houses along Nyhavn**

LONDON, NEW YORK,
MELBOURNE, MUNICH AND DELHI
www.dk.com

Reproduced by Colourscan, Singapore
Printed and bound in China by Leo Paper
Products Ltd

First published in Great Britain in 2007
by Dorling Kindersley Limited
80 Strand, London WC2R 0RL
A Penguin Company

**Copyright 2007, 2009 © Dorling
Kindersley Limited, London**

Reprinted with revisions 2009

A CIP catalogue record is available from
the British Library.

ISBN 978 1 40533 880 6

Within each Top 10 list in this book, no
hierarchy of quality or popularity is implied.
All 10 are, in the editor's opinion, of
roughly equal merit.

MIX
Paper from
responsible sources
FSC
www.fsc.org   FSC™ C018179

Contents

Copenhagen's Top 10

The information in this DK Eyewitness Top 10 Travel Guide is checked regularly.
Every effort has been made to ensure that this book is as up-to-date as possible at the time of
going to press. Some details, however, such as telephone numbers, opening hours, prices,
gallery hanging arrangements and travel information are liable to change. The publishers
cannot accept responsibility for any consequences arising from the use of this book, nor for
any material on third party websites, and cannot guarantee that any website address in this
book will be a suitable source of travel information. We value the views and suggestions of
our readers very highly. Please write to: Publisher, DK Eyewitness Travel Guides,
Dorling Kindersley, 80 Strand, London WC2R 0RL.

Left **Interior of Vor Frue Kirke** Right **Kunstindustrimuseet**

Contents

Left **New Year fireworks at Tivoli** Right **Café culture at Nytorv**

Key to abbreviations
Adm admission charge **Dis Access** disabled access

COPENHAGEN'S
TOP 10

COPENHAGEN'S TOP 10

TOP10 Copenhagen's Highlights

A kaleidoscope of history, culture and contemporary entertainment, Copenhagen is a vibrant capital city offering an incredible array of experiences. Walk through the cobbled streets of an ancient city, explore world-class museums, experience the finest restaurants and hippest nightlife, or simply unwind beside the gorgeous waters of a peaceful seaside town. Copenhagen has a compact centre which can easily be seen on foot and is also a great city for cycling. Voted "Europe's Coolest City" by design magazine Wallpaper, this charming destination has something for everyone.

Harbour Sights 1
The best way to soak in the city's plentiful and beautiful harbour sights is to take a harbour trip, from Nyhavn through the Inner Harbour, along the canals of Slotsholmen and Christianshavn. It is also a fantastic way to understand Copenhagen's development over the years.

Tivoli 2
This pleasure garden and fun fair attracts kids and adults alike. At night, it turns especially magical with sparkling fairy lights and Chinese lanterns. The rides are brilliant for an adrenaline rush and if you feel peckish, head to one of the great restaurants.

Rosenborg Slot & 3 Kongens Have
Set amid one of Copenhagen's prettiest parks, this 16th-century Renaissance castle houses the royal collection, including the spectacular Crown Jewels in the basement.

The Latin Quarter 4
One of the oldest areas in the city, the Latin Quarter is just off the main pedestrianised street, Strøget. It is home to the university and the few medieval buildings in Copenhagen.

Preceding pages: **Colourful houses lining Nyhavn.**

Kongens Nytorv and Nyhavn

Kongens Nytorv (King's New Square) is a splendid Baroque square that leads down to Nyhavn. Previously a seedy haunt for sailors, complete with drinking dens and brothels, it has transformed radically in recent times. Today, this scenic area is a popular waterside attraction with plenty of restaurants and bars.

Amalienborg

Home to the royal family since 1794, this complex of palaces represents some of the best Baroque architecture in Denmark. The museum housed in Christian VIII's palace has some fascinating displays.

Statens Museum for Kunst

You will find a wonderful collection of Danish and European sculpture and paintings at this national art museum. It is set inside a 19th-century building, connected by a glass bridge to a modern wing. There is also a pretty park behind the museum.

Ny Carlsberg Glyptotek

This fabulous, recently renovated and extended museum is a definite must-see. It includes wonderful ancient Egyptian, Roman and Mediterranean works of art. The new wing boasts an impressive collection of French Impressionist and Post-Impressionist art.

Nationalmuseet

Here is a perfect example of how brilliantly the Danes design their museums. Formerly a palace, the museum *(left)* houses collections devoted to Danish history. You will also find fabulous ethnographic artifacts from around the world, as well as an excellent children's museum.

Slotsholmen

This is where it all began in the 11th century, when Bishop Absalon built a castle here (you can still see its remains), which stood till 1794, when it burned down. The present Neo-Baroque castle was built in 1907–28, but was never inhabited by the monarch. It now houses the Parliament.

Kastellet

Amalie Haven

300 ⊢ yards ⌐ 0 ⌐ metres ⊢ 300

Harbour Sights

A harbour tour is a delightful way to take in the city's brilliant views and varied topography. You will be taken along the wide waters of the Inner Harbour, winding waterways of Christianshavn and round to Slotsholmen (the island on which the original town of Havn flourished in the 12th century). Vor Frelsers Kirke, in particular, makes a spectacular sight as you look up through the rigging of sailing boats dotting the Christianshavn canal.

Den Sorte Diamant
The Black Diamond, an eye-catching extension of the Royal Library, is a vast, shiny structure. It is home to over 4.5 million books and also houses the Queen's Hall and several exhibition spaces.

Operaen

🌀 DFDS and Netto Boats both offer guided canal and harbour tours. If you would rather not have commentary or see the canals, take a HUR Harbour Bus (901/902) from Den Sorte Diamant, Knippelsbro, Nyhavn, the Opera House, Nyholm or Larsen Plads. Copenhagen Cards are accepted *(see p111)*.

• Map L4
• DFDS Canal Tours: 32 96 30 00; open 10am–5pm; adm for adults 60kr, children 25kr; boats every 30 mins; tours in English, French, Danish and German; www.canaltours.com
• Netto Boats: 32 54 41 02; open 9:30am–5pm 15 Mar–22 Dec; adm for adults 30kr, children 15kr; boats 2–5 times an hour; tours in English, German, Danish and French; www.netto-baadene.dk

Top 10 Attractions

1. Operaen
2. Nyhavn
3. Den Sorte Diamant
4. Langelinie
5. Havnebadet
6. Little Mermaid
7. Trekroner
8. The Canals
9. Houseboats
10. Pavilions and the Royal Yacht

Operaen
The incredible Opera House *(above left)* was built in just four years. Its massive, orange-maple coloured auditorium seats 1,700 people. The amazing sculptures in the foyer change colour with the weather.

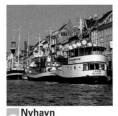

Nyhavn
Even today, the charming old harbour of Nyhavn is filled with boats. The old brothels and pubs have now been turned into respectable bars and restaurants serving traditional Danish dishes.

Langelinie
One of Copenhagen's most scenic areas, this is a wonderful place to walk along the harbour banks. Stroll past Kastellet and the Little Mermaid, right up to the final stretch – the longest cruise ship pier outside Miami *(below)*.

Inderhavnen (Inner Harbour) runs through central Copenhagen; Øresund (the Sound) separates Denmark and Sweden.

5 Havnebadet
Take a refreshing dip in the sparkling clean harbour waters of this popular open-air pool, while enjoying superb views of the city. Located at Island's Brygge, there are three pools to choose from – for adults, children and a pool for divers. They are separated from each other and from the harbour waters by floating bridges.

10 Pavilions and the Royal Yacht
On the quayside, just beyond the Little Mermaid, are two green pavilions (below). It is here that the Danish royal family gathers before boarding their stunning, 79-m (259-ft) royal yacht, called the Dannebrog, also the name of the Danish flag, which is said to have fallen from the sky in the year 1219. Launched in 1931, the yacht is crewed by nine officers, seven sergeants, and 36 seamen: an improvement on the earlier royal ship, a paddle steamer dating back to the year 1879.

8 The Canals
The canals that you glide along on the tour (above), were built in a Dutch style in 1618 at the command of Christian IV. It is because of this that Christianshavn is sometimes also referred to as "Little Amsterdam".

Mutant Mermaid

Close to the Little Mermaid, practically inviting controversy, sits a collection of sculptures called Paradise Genetically Altered. It shows a triumphal arch, with a 9-m (29-ft), genetically-altered Madonna atop it, surrounded by Adam, Eve, Christ, Mary Magdalene, The Tripartite Capital and The Pregnant Man. It is a surreal take on the Little Mermaid perched a short distance away. Designed by radical artist Bjørn Nørgaard, it is a comment on the modern human condition.

6 Little Mermaid
Den Lille Havfrue is a surprisingly small landmark, commissioned by the brewery magnate, Carl Jacobsen in 1909. The statue was created in 1913 by Edvard Eriksen, who used his wife Eline as the model.

7 Trekroner
This 18th-century fort has been used only once: on 1 April 1801, during the Battle of Copenhagen when firing against the British fleet. Second in command at that time was Admiral Lord Nelson.

9 Houseboats
The houseboats along the canals have an eclectic mix of styles, ranging from the conventional boat-like structures, to some with barge-like designs and other modern, funky homes built on floating platforms, complete with outdoor spaces.

For hotels with water views, see p117; and for days out by the Sound, see pp96–103.

🔟 Tivoli

Famous for its fairy-tale ambience, exotic buildings, gorgeous landscaped gardens and upmarket entertainment and restaurants, the Tivoli Gardens are more than an amusement park. The atmosphere is magical enough to merit a visit even if you are not interested in the excellent rides on offer. Founded in 1843, Tivoli has long been a favourite with royalty. It also proved to be a great source of inspiration for Walt Disney when he visited in 1950.

Thrill Rides
Day or night, Tivoli rings with the shrieks of people whizzing along on the high-speed thrill rides, such as *The Dragon, The Demon* and *The Starflyer,* the world's tallest carousel.

Tivoli Gardens

🍃 Go on the thrill rides during the day when it's more family-oriented, since queues can build up in the evenings.

🍴 Enjoy a meal at one of the restaurants here *(see pp12–13).*

- Map H5
- Vesterbrogade 3
- 33 15 10 01
- Open Apr–mid-Jun: 11am–11pm Sun–Thu; mid-Jun–mid-Aug: 11am–11pm Mon–Wed, 11am–midnight Thu–Fri & Sun, 11am–12:30am Sat; mid-Aug–Sep: 11am–11pm Sun–Thu, 11am–12:30am Fri, 11am–midnight Sat; mid-Nov–Dec 11am–10pm Sun–Thu, 11am–11pm Fri & Sat
- Adm for adults 85kr; children 45kr; free for under-12s
- Dis access
- www.tivoli.dk

Top 10 Features
1. Thrill Rides
2. Gentle Rides
3. Traditional Rides
4. Dragon Boats
5. Tivoli at Night
6. Pantomime Theatre
7. Tivoli Koncertsal and Open-Air Stage
8. Tivoli Akvarium
9. Tivoli Boys' Guard
10. Hotel Nimb

Gentle Rides
For children and the faint-hearted, there are plenty of fun, gentle rides. *The Blue Sapphire* is an observation wheel that offers great views over Tivoli. You could also enjoy an old-fashioned trolley bus ride, a traditional carousel with exotic animals and pipe-organ music, a merry-go-round in the shape of a Viking ship and several charming kids' rides, such as flying aeroplanes and miniature classic cars.

Traditional Rides
Tivoli's Ferris Wheels date to 1884, but the current one is from 1943. *The Mountain* (1914), the oldest roller coaster, reaches speeds of 50 mph (80.5 km/h).

Dragon Boats
4 These boats are very popular rides at Tivoli. Kids love floating on the lake during the day. In the evenings, the setting turns romantic.

Tivoli at Night
5 Sparkling resplendently with thousands of fairy lights and Chinese lanterns, Tivoli is magical at night. You can catch the dazzling *son-et-lumière* presentation and the exuberant *A Tivoli Fairytale* show, which includes a stunning display of multi-coloured fireworks.

Pantomime Theatre
6 Built in 1874, this theatre has an exotic Chinese design and a spectacular stage curtain styled like a peacock's tail *(left)*. It is known for its enjoyable mime shows, performed in the commedia dell'arte tradition.

Tivoli Koncertsal and Open-Air Stage
7 The renovated Concert Hall hosts varied performances, from classical music to pop concerts. The open-air stage holds free rock concerts on Friday nights.

Tivoli Akvarium
8 Don't miss the amazing aquarium in the foyer of the Concert Hall. Based on a tropical coral reef, it is the longest salt water aquarium in Denmark and is home to 1,600 fish (over 500 varieties). Among the popular attractions are the rays and the enormous eels.

Tivoli Boys' Guard
9 A tradition since 1844, the Boys' Guards parade through Tivoli, complete with instruments, coach and horses – a delightful picture, befitting the home city of that master of fairy tales, HC Andersen.

Hotel Nimb
10 This splendid hotel housed in the Tivoli Palace *(above)* offers a variety of culinary experiences, such as a chocolate factory, a deli store, a grill with home-made hotdogs, a gourmet restaurant and a dairy.

Christmas at Tivoli
Tivoli opens for six weeks between mid-November and the end of December for a winter wonderland; a no-holds-barred, elf-driven, ice-skating, Father Christmas-strewn, pantomime-filled, illuminated Christmas extravaganza that you won't forget in a hurry! A similar Halloween celebration is a recent innovation.

For more places that children will enjoy, see pp56–7.

Left **The Paul restaurant** Centre **Café Ketchup** Right **Café Ultimo**

🔟 Tivoli Restaurants

1 The Paul
This Michelin-starred restaurant, set in a lovely Winter Garden, is run by award-winning chef Paul Cunningham. Its six-course set menu for lunch and dinner changes regularly and includes dishes like creamed truffled pasta. ⊗ 35 75 07 75 • www.thepaul.dk • ⊗⊗⊗⊗⊗

2 Frigatten
Enjoy a sumptuous meal and superb salads on this fantastic replica of a sailing ship. In summer, you can sit out on the deck and take in the views. ⊗ 33 15 92 04 • www. bojesen.dk • ⊗⊗⊗⊗

3 Café Ultimo
Italian cuisine is served in this pretty, circular building that was originally built as a dance hall in 1883. ⊗ 33 75 07 51 • www.cafeultimotivoli.dk • ⊗⊗⊗

Det Kinesiske Tårn

4 Café Ketchup
Styled like a Parisian bistro, this lovely restaurant, formerly a 19th-century tea room, offers a variety of tantalizing fusion dishes and traditional Danish fares too. ⊗ 33 75 07 55 • www. cafeketchuptivoli.dk • ⊗⊗⊗⊗⊗

5 Divan 2
Along with Café Ketchup (formerly Divan I), this is one of the oldest and best restaurants in Tivoli, offering excellent Danish delicacies. It has played host to Queen Elizabeth II, Jimmy Carter, Henry Kissinger and Indira Gandhi. ⊗ www.divan2.dk • ⊗⊗⊗⊗⊗

6 Det Kinesiske Tårn
This exotic Tivoli icon on the lake makes a spectacular picture, especially when it is lit up at night. Choose from their Cantonese buffet, à la carte or Danish menu. ⊗ 33 33 78 00 • Chinese Buffet: 5pm–10pm • www. kinesisketaarn.dk • ⊗⊗

7 Færgekroen Bryghus
Færgekroen, one of Tivoli's oldest restaurants, has been made over into a modern space complete with its own brewery. The rustic charm has been preserved, while the traditional Danish food perfectly complements the fine home-made ales. ⊗ 33 75 06 80 • www.faergekroen.com • ⊗⊗⊗

8 Wagamama
One of Copenhagen's cheapest restaurants, this trendy chain offering excellent Japanese fare is situated in the new complex at the Tivoli Concert Hall. It can get very busy, so don't be surprised if you find yourself sharing a table with strangers. ⊗ 33 75 06 58 • www.wagamama.dk • ⊗⊗⊗

For a key to the price categories, **see pp67, 71, 79, 87, 93 and 103.**

9 Hereford Beefstouw

The flagship restaurant in a chain of upmarket steakhouses, the Hereford Beefstouw is a mecca for people who love beef and beer. The steaks are cooked just right and are of first-class quality with prices to match. Its micro-brewery, the Apollo, stands right in the centre of the restaurant.

Stegt Flæsk

🔗 Vesterbrogade 5 • 33 12 74 41 • Open 11:30am–3pm & 5:30pm–10:30pm Mon–Sat, 5pm–10:30pm Sun • www.a-h-b.dk/tivoli • ⊗⊗⊗⊗

10 La Vecchia Signora

This cheerful Italian restaurant is well known for its stone-oven-baked pizzas, all produced in traditional ovens specially imported from Sardinia, Italy. The rest of the menu includes homemade pasta topped with a variety of sauces, *carpaccio*, mussels in parsley and garlic, fresh fish of the day, meat dishes and authentic Italian puddings. 🔗 33 75 09 75 • Children's menu available • ⊗⊗⊗

Top 10 Historic Events

1 1843: Tivoli opens with a horse-drawn carousel and a roller coaster.

2 1944: The Nazis blow up part of Tivoli in order to crush Danish morale.

3 1950: Walt Disney visits Tivoli and is inspired to create his own park.

4 1956: The Concert Hall is inaugurated, the largest one in Northern Europe at the time.

5 1978: The New York City Ballet and its founder, George Balanchine, visit.

6 1990s: Michael Jackson performs at Tivoli and offers to buy it.

7 1994: Tivoli's Christmas season is launched.

8 2000: Hosts the 60th birthday celebrations for the Queen.

9 2003: The Paul, Tivoli's first Michelin-starred restaurant, opens.

10 2006: Launch of *The Starflyer*, the world's tallest carousel.

The Founding of Tivoli

The creation of the Tivoli Gardens can be credited to Georg Carstensen, a man who persuaded the Danish king, Christian VIII, to grant him a five-year charter by saying, "When the people are amusing themselves, they do not think about politics." Mindful of this fact, Christian VIII granted him 6 ha (15 acres) of land outside the city walls. Carstensen, who had been brought up in the Middle East, provided oriental-style buildings, cafés, restaurants and in the early days, a horse-drawn carousel and a roller coaster. Brilliant fireworks further enlivened this magnificent amusement area. It was named Tivoli after the Jardins de Tivoli in Paris, which were themselves named after a place called Tivoli just outside Rome. The gardens inspired Walt Disney greatly when he visited; in fact, he was so impressed by them he once exclaimed to his wife, "Now this is what an amusement place should be!"

Tivoli at night

For more restaurants in the Tivoli area, see pp67 and 71.

Rosenborg Slot and Kongens Have

Complete with fairy-tale turrets and stone lions guarding the entrance, the Rosenborg Castle was originally built as a summer house in 1606–34 by Christian IV. At that time, it stood surrounded by sprawling gardens (now the Kongens Have park) out in the tranquil countryside. This was Christian IV's favourite castle and like other monarchs after him, he used it as his main residence. When he was on his deathbed at Frederiksberg Castle in 1648, he insisted on being brought to Rosenborg Castle, and eventually died here.

Rosenborg Slot

🛈 Avoid lurking near the guards at the entrance to the Crown Jewels – you might be considered a security risk.

🍴 There is a restaurant and a small café in Kongens Have, but you will enjoy yourself a lot more if you have a picnic on the lawn or on one of the many benches in the garden.

• Map J2
• Øster Voldgade 4A
• 33 15 32 86
• Open Nov–Apr 11am–4pm Tue–Sun; May–Oct 10am–4pm daily
• Adm for adults 65kr, students and senior citizens 40kr, free for under-17s; Kongens Have gardens free; Copenhagen Card accepted (see p111)
• Guided tours (1–1.5 hr long) in English, German and French
• museum@dkks.dk
• www.rosenborgslot.dk

Top 10 Features

1 Rosenborg Slot
2 Crown Jewels
3 The Winter Room
4 Christian IV's Bedroom
5 The Dark Room
6 The Marble Hall
7 Frederik IV's Chamber Room
8 The Rosen Antechamber
9 Knight's Hall
10 Kongens Have

Rosenborg Slot

The castle's 24 rooms occupy three floors. Most of them retain the original Renaissance decor from Christian IV's residence, while the rest have been redecorated by later kings. The last king to live here permanently was Frederik IV. The castle is unique for its museum tradition, which started during the Dano-Swedish wars in 1657–60.

Crown Jewels

The castle has been used as the treasury of the realm since 1658. In the castle's basement, behind heavily-guarded security doors, are Denmark's Crown Jewels *(above)*, that include Christian IV's diamond-encrusted crown, pearls and enamel figures.

The Winter Room

This panelled room was said to be one of Christian IV's most important private chambers. Look out for the intriguing speaking tubes that connect with the wine cellar and room above.

Christian IV's Bedroom

Another private apartment, Christian IV's bloodied clothing, from the naval battle of Kolberger Heide (1644) where he lost an eye, are found here. The king wanted these clothes preserved as national mementos.

Share your travel recommendations on traveldk.com

The Dark Room

This room is filled with fascinating objects, such as the startling wax portraits of the Absolute monarchs, and the 17th-century "trick" chair that grasped unsuspecting occupants with tentacles and soaked them in water. A trumpet played when they finally stood up.

The Marble Hall

Originally the bedroom of Kirsten Munk, Christian IV's morganatic wife, Frederik III turned it into a Baroque show of splendour *(below)* to celebrate the introduction of Absolute Monarchy.

Frederik IV's Chamber Room

In the 1700s, this room was used by Frederik IV's sister, Sophie Hedvig, as an antechamber and the tapestries date back to this period. Look for the intricate equestrian statue of Frederik, made from ivory, wood and tortoise shell. The coffered ceiling *(below)* is the original from the time of Christian IV.

The Rosen Antechamber

An extraordinary room with glowing gold leaves and tooled leather on the walls, it has undergone restoration to look exactly as it did before the royal family shifted to Frederiksberg Slot around the 1740s. The room's square shape has since been restored and the fittings, ceiling paintings and wall decorations were brought back from Frederiksberg Slot.

Knight's Hall

Previously known as the Long Hall (before 1750), this room was completed in 1624 as a celebration hall. Only two Dutch fireplaces remain from the original decorations. Note the beautiful white stucco ceiling, Frederik III's astonishing unicorn horn throne (1660s) and the solid-silver, Baroque furniture.

Kongens Have

Visited by over two million people every year, these are Denmark's oldest royal gardens and date back to the 17th century. There is a rose garden, Staudehaven, which contains many statues including one of Hans Christian Andersen and a large one of Queen Caroline Amalie that was created by Vilhelm Bissen. Enjoy a lovely long walk on the pathway that passes through the flowerbeds. A new addition to the park is the Renaissance garden, Krumspringet. Art events and puppet theatre for children are held here during summer.

Rosenborg's Kings

Christian IV, 1588–1648: Built many of Copenhagen's Renaissance buildings.
Frederik III, 1648–1670: Introduced Absolute Monarchy to curb the aristocracy's power.
Christian V, 1670–1699: Introduced fairer taxation.
Frederik IV, 1699–1730: Built Frederiksberg Castle, among other well-known buildings.
Christian VI, 1730–1746: Known as the religious king.
Frederik V, 1746–1766: Founded the Royal Danish Academy of Art.

For more royal sights, see **pp58–9.**

10 The Latin Quarter

The Latin Quarter is home to Copenhagen's university, where Latin used to be the spoken language. One of the oldest areas in the city, it is full of 17th-century buildings that were built by the architect king, Christian IV. Although there have been dwellings here since medieval times, most of them were destroyed in the disastrous fire that spread across Copenhagen in 1728 (see p40). Today, the Latin Quarter is a lively and bustling student area brimming with shops and cafés.

Universitetet

🌀 This area is known for its hip, alternative shops.

🔵 Studenterhuset, opposite Regensen, is a cheap option.

- Map H4
- Hellingåndskirken: Niels Hemmingsensgade 5; 33 15 41 44; open 12pm–4pm Mon–Sat.
- Synagogen: Krystalgade 12; 33 12 88 68
- Rundetårn, Trinitatis Kirke: Købmagergade 52A; 33 73 03 73; Tower: open Jun–Aug 10am–8pm Mon–Sat, noon–5pm Sun; Sep–May 10am–5pm Mon–Sat, noon–5 pm Sun; www.rundetårn.dk Church: open 9:30am–4:30pm Mon–Sat; www.trinitatiskirke.dk
- Universitetet: Nørregade 10; 35 32 26 26; open 9am–5pm daily; www.ku.dk/english/
- Vor Frue Kirke: Nørregade 8; open 10am–noon Mon–Sat
- Sankt Petri Kirke: Skt Peders St 2; 33 13 38 33; open 10am–noon Sun

Top 10 Features

1. Helligåndskirken
2. Synagogen
3. Rundetårn
4. Universitetet
5. Trinitatis Kirke
6. Vor Frue Kirke
7. Sankt Petri Kirke
8. Regensen
9. Højbro Plads
10. Gråbrødretorv

Helligåndskirken

The Church of the Holy Ghost *(below)* was originally part of a monastery built in 1296 and dissolved in 1536. The Helligåndshuset, the monastery's west wing, is the city's only preserved medieval building.

Synagogen

Built in 1833, this is Copenhagen's oldest synagogue, and one of the few in Europe to have survived Nazi occupation. The main synagogue for the city's Jewish community, it is not open to visitors.

Rundetårn

The Round Tower was built in 1642 by Christian IV as an observatory, its official role till 1861. It is now open to the public *(see p36).* It is 34.8 m (114 ft) high, with a wide internal ramp that spirals almost to the top *(below).* It also holds art exhibitions and classical concerts.

Tsar Peter of Russia supposedly rode his horse to the top of the Rundetårn in 1715, his wife following in a coach and six.

Universitetet

Founded in 1479 by Christian I, this was Denmark's first university. The Neo-Classical building that stands here today is from the 19th century. In the courtyard, there are the remains of an old Bishop's Palace (1420). Disorderly students used to be placed in its cellar as punishment. Most of the university is now on the island of Amager.

Trinitatis Kirke

This magnificent church was built in 1637–57 for the staff and students of the university. If it happens to be closed when you visit, you could enter Rundetårn and look down the church nave through the glass panel at the start of the ramp.

Vor Frue Kirke

In the 12th century, Bishop Absalon founded a Gothic church on this site. After burning down twice, the present Neo-Classical building was completed in 1829, but the tower is from medieval times. One of the bells is Denmark's oldest (1490) and another (weighing 4 tonnes) is the biggest.

Sankt Petri Kirke

Older than Vor Frue Kirke, this church also suffered from city fires and the British bombardment (1807). It has a vaulted sepulchral chapel with monuments and tombs that date back to 1681–83.

Regensen

Opposite the Rundetårn, this student residence was built in the 17th century. It burned down in the great fire of 1728, but was rebuilt in the same year. Even today, the students retain several old traditions, including "storming" Rundetårn every May.

Højbro Plads

The equestrian statue on this popular square depicts Bishop Absalon, founder of Copenhagen, pointing towards the site of his original castle on Slotsholmen.

Gråbrødretorv

Named after the Grey Brothers who built Copenhagen's first monastery here, this 13th-century square is now a popular place to eat in the open air.

The Bells and Carillion of Helligåndskirken

In 1647, 50 years after the clock tower was built, architect king Christian IV gifted the church a set of bells and a grand carillion. The carillion consisted of 19 bells and chimed a verse from a hymn every 30 minutes. It was also used at funerals; the importance of the deceased depended on the duration for which it played. This was at times taken too far, as playwright Ludwig Holberg (1684–1754) said when the carillion played for four straight hours: "A soul need not be so long on its way to heaven as the mail horse is to Roskilde". They were destroyed in the fire of 1728.

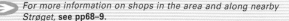

For more information on shops in the area and along nearby Strøget, see pp68–9.

TOP 10 Kongens Nytorv and Nyhavn

Kongens Nytorv (King's New Square) and Nyhavn (New Harbour) are two of the most picturesque areas in Copenhagen. It's hard to imagine the square was once outside the city gates and the site of the town gallows in medieval times. The Nyhavn canal was planned by Frederik III to connect the Inner Harbour with the square, enabling merchants to unload their goods more easily. The canal area is full of chic, colourful houses and charming bars. In winter, you will also find a popular skating rink here.

Equestrian statue

✪ The bars and restaurants to the south of Nyhavn are usually not as busy as those on the north.

◉ If you are looking for a quick bite away from the crowds, check out the Thomas Sandwich shop at 14 Lille Strandstræde.

• Map K4–L4
• Charlottenborg Slot: Nyhavn 2; 33 11 11 91; open noon–9pm Tue–Thu, noon–5pm Fri–Sun; adm 60kr, seniors and students 40kr; www.charlottenborg-art.dk
• Amber Museum: Kongens Nytorv 2; 33 11 67 00; open May–Sep 10am–8pm daily, Oct–Apr 10am–6pm daily
• Magasin du Nord: Kongens Nytorv 13; open 10am–7pm Mon–Sat (to 8pm Fri, to 5pm Sat); www.magasin.dk
• Det Kongelige Teater: Kongens Nytorv; 33 69 69 33; open noon–8pm Mon–Sat, closed annual summer break; adm 75kr; www.kglteater.dk

Top 10 Features

1. Nyhavn
2. Nyhavn Nos 20, 67 and 18
3. Equestrian Statue
4. Hotel d' Angleterre
5. Charlottenborg Slot
6. Det Kongelige Teater
7. Magasin du Nord
8. Vingårdsstræde 6
9. Store Strandestræde and Lille Strandstræde
10. Amber Museum

Nyhavn
Running down to the Inner Harbour, this canal is flanked by 18th-century houses that belonged to merchants. A large anchor, in honour of sailors who lost their lives in Word War II, marks the starting point of Nyhavn.

Nyhavn Nos 20, 67, 18
These brightly painted merchants' houses were built at the same time as the harbour. Fairy-tale writer, HC Andersen, has lived in all. He wrote his first tale, *The Tinder Box* (1835), at No 20.

Equestrian Statue
This bronze statue in the middle of Kongens Nytorv commemorates Christian V (1646–99) who rebuilt the square in 1670 in Neo-Classical style. Sculpted by the Frenchman Lamoureux, it shows the king dressed as a Roman emperor.

Hotel d'Angleterre
Copenhagen's oldest hotel (1775), it has played host to royalty and countless celebrities. When Michael Jackson visited, he was so impressed with a suit of armour outside the Royal Suite, he offered to buy the entire hotel.

For more sights associated with HC Andersen, see pp38–9.

Charlottenborg Slot

An early example of the Danish Baroque style, this palace *(right)* was built by Frederik III's illegitimate son Ulrik in 1672–83. It has belonged to the Royal Academy since 1734 and often holds interesting exhibitions. If you walk along the north side of Nyhavn, you will get a better view of the palace walls and also find an entrance into its courtyard.

Det Kongelige Teater

This Baroque-style theatre is the third one to stand on this site since 1749. It is home to the Royal Theatre Company and the Royal Ballet.

Vingårdsstræde 6

HC Andersen lived in this attic room for a year at the age of 22. You can enter the room from the third floor of the Magasin du Nord *(see right)*. No 6 is one of the oldest buildings in Copenhagen. Its 13th-century wine cellars (there used to be a vineyard here, hence *Vingårdsstræde*) now house a Michelin-starred restaurant.

Store Strandstræde and Lille Strandstræde

Once full of seedy pubs and brothels, "Big Beach Street" and "Little Beach Street" are now home to art galleries and stylish designer wear shops *(left)*. For a taste of its past, there are a couple of tattoo parlours down Store Strandstræde.

Amber Museum

Set in a house dating back to 1606, this museum *(right)* displays an exquisite collection dedicated to Denmark's national gem, amber (also called Nordic Gold). You will find amber antiques, pre-historic pieces and a 8.8-kg (19-lb) amber stone. Amber jewellery is also sold at a shop on the premises.

Magasin du Nord

Originally the famous Hotel du Nord, this is Copenhagen's oldest department store *(left)* and is considered to be the city's answer to London's Selfridges or New York's Bloomingdale's. Standing to the north side of the Kongens Nytorv, the store will strike you as an impressive sight when you pass by. A variety of restaurants are scattered throughout the building. Make sure you pay a visit to the Food Hall that is housed in the basement of the department store. It features on its menu a wide variety of delicious preparations that are worth sampling.

"The Imperial Ethiopian Palace" in Copenhagen

In the 1950s, Ethopia's Emperor Haile Selassie (also known as the King of Kings or the Conquering Lion of the Tribe of Judah), his wife and their entire family and entourage, visited Denmark's king and queen. In Copenhagen for only a few days, they stayed at the plush and luxurious Hotel d'Angleterre. A grand banquet was held in honour of Denmark's royal visitors in the Louis XVI Hall. During the time of their stay in the hotel, all telephone calls were answered with, "The Imperial Ethiopian Palace".

🔟 Amalienborg and Frederiksstaden

Built in the 1750s, this stately complex was designed by the royal architect, Nicolas Eigtved. Four Rococo palaces, originally home to four noble families, are set around an octagonal square in Frederiksstaden, an artistocratic area built by Frederik V. The king bought the palaces after the Christiansborg Palace burned down in 1794. The royal family has lived here ever since. It was named after a palace built on this site by Queen Sophie Amalie in the 17th century, which burned down in 1689 during a theatrical performance.

Amaliehaven

🕐 The guards will not respond well to people sitting on palace steps.

🍴 Head down Amaliegade to the bars and cafés along Nyhavn.

• Map L3
• Christian VII's Palace: 33 92 64 51; guided tours only Jul–mid-Sep 1pm & 2:30pm in English; adm 75kr
• Christian VIII's Palace: 33 12 21 86; open Nov–Apr 11am–4pm Tue–Sun, May–Oct 10am–4pm daily; adm for adults 50kr, students 30kr, free with Copenhagen Card; www.amalienborg museet.dk
• Marmorkirken: Frederiksgade 4; 33 15 01 44; open 10am–7pm Mon–Thu, noon–5pm Fri–Sun; www. marmorkirken.dk

Top 10 Features

1. Christian VII's Palace
2. Christian VIII's Palace
3. Frederik VIII's Palace
4. Christian IX's Palace
5. Equestrian Statue of Frederik V
6. Marmorkirken
7. Amaliehaven
8. Palace Guards
9. The Golden Axis
10. The Colonade

Christian VIII's Palace

This is where Crown Prince Frederik lived until his marriage to Australian Mary Donaldson in 2004. Part of the palace is open all year round as a museum that is dedicated to the Glücksberg Dynasty. Visit Queen Louise's chintzy drawing room and the studies of several kings.

1 Christian VII's Palace

This palace was one of the first to be completed by the time of Eigtved's death in 1754. Also known as Moltke Palace, named after its original owner, Lord Adam Gottlob Moltke, it is the most expensive palace in the complex and also has one of Denmark's best Rococo interiors. The queen often uses it to welcome foreign guests.

Marmorkirken

3 Frederik VIII's Palace

Previously known as Brockdorff's Palace, this palace *(left)* with a clock on its façade was renamed after Frederik VIII moved into it in 1869. More recently, it was home to Queen Dowager Ingrid (Queen Margrethe's mother) till her death in 2000. It is currently the residence of Crown Prince Frederik and Crown Princess Mary.

4 Christian IX's Palace

The first royal family to live here was Crown Prince Frederik IV and his wife (1794). Since 1967, it has been home to Queen Margrethe and Prince Consort Henrik.

5 Equestrian Statue of Frederik V

Designed and cast (1753–71) by French sculptor Jacques Saly, this statue of Frederik V is said to have cost four times as much as the Amalienborg. Saly, who stayed here for 18 years, was known for the extravagant parties he hosted. His expenses were paid by the Danish Asiatic Company, who gifted this statue to the king.

6 Marmorkirken

Properly called Frederikskirken, the Marble Church *(left)* got its popular name on account of plans to build it using Norwegian marble. Its dome, one of the largest in Europe and modelled after St Peter's in Rome, has a diameter of 31 m (102 ft).

7 Amaliehaven

The Amalie Garden was created in 1993 on the banks of the Harbour, financed by the shipping giant AP Møller and the Christine McKinney Møller Foundation. It has a splendid fountain that lies on Copenhagen's "Golden Axis" *(see below)*, between the Opera House and the statue of Frederik V.

8 Palace Guards

When the queen is in residence, the Danish Royal Life Guards *(right)* stand outside the palace, guarding their monarch in two-hour shifts. At noon they are replaced by the guards from Rosenborg Castle *(pp14–15)*, who march through the streets of Copenhagen every day at 11:30am to switch places with the guards at Amalienborg Palace.

9 The Golden Axis

The Marble Church and Frederiksstaden lie on a short axis called the Golden Axis. This axis was considered so important that when the Opera House was built along this line, it caused much controversy. The building is now considered the axis' modern extension.

10 The Colonnade

This Classical-style colonnade was built by Christian VII's royal architect, Caspar Frederik Harsdorff in 1794–95. Supported by eight ionic columns, it runs unobtrusively from one palace to another along the first-floor level.

The Russian Connection

A stone's throw from Marmorkirken, the golden onion domes of Alexander Nevsky Kirke, the Russian Orthodox Cathedral, are easily identifiable *(see p78)*. Consecrated in 1883, it was a gift from the future Tsar Alexander III to mark his marriage to the Danish Princess Marie Dagmar in St Petersburg in 1866. It was in this church that her funeral was held when she passed away in 1928.

Christian IX was called the "Father-in-law of Europe"; his children married into royal families from Sweden, Britain and Germany.

Statens Museum for Kunst

Denmark's national gallery is housed in two buildings – one dating back to the 19th century and the other, a stylish, modern extension, linked by a bridge over a sculpture gallery known as Sculpture Street. The museum's collections span international and national paintings, sculptures, installations, prints and drawings from the 14th century to the present. The national collection specialises in paintings from the Golden Age and by later 19th-century artists such as the Skagen school, the rebels of their time.

The modern extension

⚫ The children's museum provides activities every Saturday and Sunday through the summer holidays.

The department of prints and drawings has fascinating works dating back to the 15th century, including those by Rembrandt, Manet and Picasso.

⚫ The bright, stylish museum café looks out onto Østre Anlæg Lake. In good weather, the park is good for a picnic.

- Map J2
- Sølvgade 48–50
- 33 74 84 94
- Open 10am–5pm Thu–Tue, 10am–8pm Wed
- Guided tours for families are also available
- Adm for adults 80kr, concessions 50–60kr, under 18 years free; Copenhagen Card accepted (see p111)
- smk@smk.dk
- www.smk.dk

Top 10 Features

1. Sculpture Street
2. Christ as the Suffering Redeemer
3. The Meeting of Joachim and Anne
4. Portrait of Bellini
5. The Judgement of Solomon
6. Boys Bathing in Skagen
7. Portrait of Madame Matisse
8. Alice
9. The Wheel of Life
10. The Earth Weeps

Sculpture Street

This impressive, varied collection of sculptures runs the entire length of the building. The displays look resplendent beneath the sunlight streaming in through the glass roof. Don't miss Sørensen's extraordinary display of ferocious dogs.

Christ as the Suffering Redeemer

This striking painting (1495–1500) by prominent Renaissance artist Andrea Mantegna shows the Resurrection of Christ on the third day after his crucifixion. Mantegna is known for his profound interest in ancient Roman civilization; in this painting *(left)*, it comes through with the porphyry sarcophagus.

The Meeting of Joachim and Anne Outside the Golden Gate

This painting (1497) by Filippino Lippi reveals an interest in classical antiquity and the influence of Botticelli.

4 Portrait of the Venetian painter Giovanni Bellini

This portrait of Giovanni Bellini, official painter for the Venetian Republic, is an early work (1511–12) by the Venetian artist Tiziano Vecellio (better known as Titian).

5 The Judgement of Solomon

This painting by Rubens depicts the inspiring story from the Old Testament, where the wisdom of King Solomon is tested. The interplay of colours is an important part of the drama. Though created by Rubens, much of the brushwork was done by assistants.

6 Boys Bathing in Skagen, Summer Evening

This intriguing painting *(left)* by Peder S. Krøyer *(see p35)* shows three little boys playing on the beach in the moonlight. It was submitted to the World Exhibition held in Paris in 1900.

Key

- ■ Ground floor
- ■ First floor
- ■ Second floor

7 Portrait of Madame Matisse

Also known as *The Green Stripe*, this painting by Henri Matisse of his wife was to have far-reaching repercussions in the art world. It was one of several radical paintings in the 1905 *Salon d'Automne* and helped give rise to the Fauvist movement known for its bright colours and spontaneous style.

8 Alice

One of over 300 portraits by Amedeo Modigliani painted between 1915 and 1920, this beautiful painting reflects the artist's interest in African sculpture. He has made use of simple shapes and stylised features to create an idealised portrait.

9 The Wheel of Life

Belonging to the *Suite of Seasons* series, this painting (1953) by Asger Jorn *(see p35)* represents the month of January. Alluding to the medieval concept of "the wheel of life", Jorn, who was suffering from tuberculosis, was inspired to paint this in the hope for better health.

10 The Earth Weeps

This powerful painting (1981) by award-winning Danish painter, Svend Wiig Hansen, reflects the artist's early life amidst widespread violence, fear and misery, especially during the Spanish Civil War and World War II. The theme of violence is a constant feature in most of his work.

Museum Guide

Situated within the public park of Østre Anlæg, visitors can enter the museum from the corner of Sølvgade and Øster Voldgade. Buy tickets in the lobby, which is flanked by temporary exhibitions and a bookshop. The ground floor is taken up by Sculpture Street, with international art in the new extension on the first floor. The old main building houses modern Danish art.

Ny Carlsberg Glyptotek

This marvellous glyptotek (which means "a collection of statues") is set inside two 19th-century buildings linked by a charming Winter Garden and a modern wing designed by architect Henning Larsen. It holds the world-class collect-ions of Carl Jacobsen (see p84) and his son Helge, as well as some recent additions. Exhibits range from ancient Greek, Roman and Egyptian statuary, to early 19th- and 20th-century Danish and French paintings. The roof terrace affords great views of the roller coaster at Tivoli.

Dahlerup building façade

- Guided tours in English and Danish are held in the summer at 2pm on Wednesdays. Free tickets can be picked up at the museum shop; no advance booking.

- The Winter Garden has a pleasant café, which isn't too expensive. Otherwise, you can picnic discreetly on roof terrace of the new wing.

- Map H6
- Dantes Plads 7
- 33 41 81 41
- Open 10am–4pm Tue–Sun
- Adm for adults 50kr, free on Sun, under 18 years free; Copenhagen Card accepted (see p111)
- info@glyptoteket.dk
- www.glyptoteket.dk

Top 10 Features

1. The Mediterranean Collection
2. The Greek Collection
3. The Roman Collection
4. The Egyptian Collection
5. The Danish Painting Collection
6. The French Impressionists
7. The Post-Impressionists
8. 19th-century Danish Sculpture
9. 19th-century French Sculpture
10. The Winter Garden

Key

- Ground floor
- First floor
- Second floor

1 The Mediterranean Collection

Located in the new wing of the museum, this collection has fascinating artifacts from the Middle East and Etruria. One of the most impressive pieces is an ancient Etruscan sarcophagus dating back to the period between 200–150 BC.

2 The Greek Collection

The collection *(left)* has works of art from the 9th–1st centuries BC. A highlight is one of the earliest Attic healing-god reliefs (around 420 BC), which depicts a daughter of Hygeia, god of healing, promising health to Athenians during a plague. There is also a rare and beautiful marble portrait bust of Alexander the Great.

3 The Roman Collection

There are some excellent busts of Rome's public figures in this collection, including those of luminaries such as General Pompey, Emperor Augustus, the evil and depraved Caligula and Emperor Hadrian, considered to be one of the best rulers of the empire.

The Egyptian Collection
Much of this collection is displayed in fabulous underground chambers into which you descend, as if in a mummy's tomb. There are also some huge sculptures *(left)*, like that of the god Ptah (1290–1224 BC). The oldest piece is a small, 3,000-year old hippo.

The Danish Painting Collection
Here you will find great works of art from Denmark's Golden Age (1800–50), a period when art and culture blossomed despite political and economic strife. The greatest artists of the period, Eckersberg, Købke and Lundbye are especially well represented.

The French Impressionists
This collection includes paintings by Manet, Renoir, Sisley, Monet and Pissarro, among a host of other artists. The *Absinthe Drinker* by Manet is a particular highlight, as is the remarkable Degas bronze ballerina *(right)*.

The Post-Impressionists
This splendid gallery holds early works of artists like Van Gogh *(right)*, Cézanne and Lautrec, and the world's largest collection of Gauguin paintings.

19th-century Danish Sculpture
Includes works by Denmark's Neo-Classical sculptors, like Villhelm Bissen and Jens Jerichau. Bissen's *Danaid* (1880), epitomises Neo-Classical style.

19th-century French Sculpture
This stunning collection features the biggest names in French sculpture, including Rodin, Barye, Maillol Carpeaux, Dubois and Falguière.

The Winter Garden
This glass-domed garden is a great place to relax amid statues, including a replica of *The Water Mother* (1921), by Danish sculptor Kai Nielsen.

Museum Guide
Enter the museum from HC Andersens Boulevard. Buy tickets downstairs and walk straight ahead to the Winter Garden. On the right is the entrance to the Larsen building and the French Impressionist collection. Walk through the Winter Garden and up a few steps to the grand Central Hall to find the collection of Greek, Roman and Egyptian antiquities, and 19th-century Danish and French art, which continues on the second floor as well.

凸10 Nationalmuseet

The National Museum presents the history and culture of the Danes from prehistoric times to the present. It also houses a wonderful collection of Greek and Egyptian antiquities, an ethnographic collection and is also the keeper of the Royal Collection of Coins and Medals. Many of the displays derive from King Frederik III's Royal Cabinet of Curiosities put together around 1650. The state collection has had several homes and is currently housed in the Prince's Palace at Frederiksholms Kanal, where it has been since the 1850s.

The museum atrium

🞇 **The Victorian Home**, a plush apartment with authentic 19th-century interiors, owned by the museum, is also located nearby.

🞇 Visit the museum café on the second floor, or go to **Ny Carlsberg Glyptotek** *(see pp24–5)*, for lunch in the Winter Garden.

- Map J5
- Ny Vestergade 10
- 33 13 44 11
- Open 10am–5pm Tue–Sun
- Free guided tours in English, Jun 11am Sun; Jul–Sep 11am every Tue, Thu and Sun
- Call for details of activities in the Children's Museum
- Guided tours of the Victorian Home (in Danish): noon, 1pm, 2pm Tue–Sun; adm for adults 50kr, concessions 40kr, free for under-18s
- www.natmus.dk

Top 10 Features

1. The Sun Chariot
2. Oak Burial Coffins
3. Gundestrup Cauldron
4. State Rooms
5. Inuit Culture
6. China, Japan and the Far East
7. Prehistoric Denmark and the Viking Age
8. Room 117
9. Cylinder Perspective Table
10. Denmark's Oldest Coin

Key

▪ Ground floor
▪ First floor
▪ Second floor
▪ Third floor

1 The Sun Chariot

The unique Sun Chariot or *Solvognen (right)*, a masterpiece of casting, was dug up in 1902 by a farmer ploughing his field. This 3,400-year-old artifact from the Bronze Age shows a horse on wheels pulling a large sun disk, gilded only on one side to represent its daytime trajectory.

2 Oak Burial Coffins

Seven oak, Bronze-Age coffins, dating back to 1,400 BC, occupy space on the ground floor. The Egtved grave, holding the body of a well-preserved, fully clad young woman is an extraordinary exhibit.

3 Gundestrup Cauldron

Found near Gundestrup, this silver cauldron *(right)* from the Iron Age, is decorated with animals and mystical figures.

4 State Rooms

The State Rooms date back to the time when this building was a royal palace. They are virtually intact from the period 1743–44; the Great Hall is adorned with the original Flemish tapestries to this day.

5 Inuit Culture
This collection *(left)* from Greenland showcases the astonishing skill and creative ingenuity from the frozen North. The displays include clothing like embroidered anoraks and boots, assorted toys and watercolours of daily life.

6 China, Japan and the Far East
The Far East is well represented in this marvellous collection that includes Japanese laquerwork, fabulously costumed Samurai warriors, replete with weaponry and beautiful 18th-century Imperial Dragon robes, worn by the Chinese emperor.

7 Prehistoric Denmark and the Viking Age
This comprehensive display of the country's 14,000-year history reopened to much acclaim in 2008. These intricate golden horns *(right)*, reconstructed in the 20th century after the 400 BC originals were melted down in 1802, are a definite highlight.

8 Room 117
This 18th-century bourgeois interior can be traced to the town of Aalborg in Jutland. A wood-panelled room in a sea of glass-display galleries, it features a heavy wooden four-poster bed, chest, coffered wooden ceiling and mullioned windows.

9 Cylinder Perspective Table
In Room 126, this table is a part of Frederik III's Royal Cabinet of Curiosities. The table top shows him and his wife, Sophie Amalie, painted ingeniously in a distorted perspective: it gets rectified when viewed in the reflective surface of a cylinder at the centre of the table.

10 Denmark's Oldest Coin
The name of Denmark and an image of a Danish king were first depicted on this small silver coin *(left)* – found in Room 144 – that was struck in AD 995.

Museum Guide
Fronted by a courtyard, the museum's entrance hall has lavatories and lockers. You can pick up a map and information in the atrium straight ahead. The museum shop, also located here, sells some interesting books and educational toys with a Viking twist. The Children's Museum is to your left. If you are time-bound, opt for the one-hour themed itineraries. The prehistoric collection is on the ground floor, while the first floor holds a range of collections, including one on ethnography. The second floor includes a history of Denmark collection (from 1660 to 2000). The antiquities are found on the third floor.

🔟 Slotsholmen

The small fishing village of Copenhagen was founded on the island of Slotsholmen in the 11th century. Bishop Absalon, the king's friend and supporter, built a castle here in 1167. Two centuries later, the castle was destroyed by the Hanseatic League, the European trade alliance that resented Copenhagen's increasing control over trade. Christiansborg Palace, which stands here today, is home to the Danish Parliament, the Jewish Museum and the Palace Church.

The Palace Church

🍴 Visit the restaurants on Gammel Strand and Højbro Plads.

- Map J5
- Christiansborg Slot: 33 92 64 92; guided tours of State Rooms May–Sep 3pm daily; Oct–Apr 3pm Tue–Sun; adm; www.ses.dk
- Ruins: open May–Sep 10am–4pm daily; Oct–Apr 10am–4pm Tue–Sun
- Stable Museum: 33 40 26 76; open 2pm–4pm Sat–Sun; May–Sep 2pm–4pm Fri also; adm
- Det Kongelige Bibliotek: adm; www.kb.dk
- Christiansborg Slotskirke: open noon–4pm Sun
- Tøjhusmuseet: 33 11 60 37; open noon–4pm Tue–Sun; weeks 7, 8, 42 & Jul 10am–4pm daily; adm; free with Copenhagen Card; www.thm.dk
- Thorvaldsens Museum: Bertel Thorvaldsens Plads 2; 33 32 15 32; open 10am–5pm Tue–Sun; adm; free with Copenhagen Card

Top 10 Features

1. Christiansborg Slot
2. Ruins Under the Palace
3. Teatermuseet
4. Stable Museum
5. Det Kongelige Bibliotek
6. Tøjhusmuseet
7. Dansk Jødisk Museum
8. Christiansborg Palace Church
9. Thorvaldsens Museum
10. Folketinget

Christiansborg Slot

Designed in a Neo-Baroque style in 1907–28 *(right)*, this sturdy construction is built from reinforced concrete and granite-lined façades. It houses the state rooms, the Folketinget (the elected parliament), the Prime Minister's apartment and the High Court. The 106-m (350-ft) high tower is the tallest one in the city.

Ruins Under The Palace

These fascinating ruins were discovered during the construction of the present palace. You can see parts of Bishop Absalon's castle *(see p65)* and the second castle that stood here until the 18th century. You will also find interesting details of the routine of daily life, such as a baker's oven, latrine chutes and hollow tree trunks used as underground pipes.

Teatermuseet

This delightful royal theatre is a part of Christian VI's Palace that escaped the fire of 1794 *(see p35)*. You can walk around the entire theatre, including the stage. The atmosphere is enhanced by classical music, mannequins in court dresses and subtle lighting.

Stable Museum

The stables *(below)* of Christian VI's Palace also survived the fire of 1794. The queen's horses are still kept here amid splendid marble walls, columns and mangers. There is also a collection of royal coaches and riding gear.

Det Kongelige Bibliotek

The Royal Library *(right)* holds all the books ever published in Denmark (4.5 million) – the biggest collection in Northern Europe. It is a great place to check out original texts by Danish authors.

Tøjhusmuseet

Housed in the arsenal built by Christian IV in 1604–08, the Royal Defense Museum is filled with artillery guns. The Armoury Hall on the first floor has 7,000 hand weapons, some from the 1300s.

Dansk Jødisk Museum

Opened in 2004, this museum *(below)* has a striking modern interior, designed by architect Daniel Libeskind. This small building brilliantly depicts the lives and culture of the Jewish population in Denmark.

Christiansborg Slotskirke

Standing on the site of the first palace church destroyed in the infamous fire of 1794 *(see p35)*, this Neo-Classical church with warm, yellow walls was built in 1813–26. However, a fire broke out in 1992 and destroyed its roof, dome and even parts of the interior. A service is held here every October for the opening of Parliament.

Thorvaldsens Museum

This orange-walled museum is home to almost all of Bertel Thorvaldsen's works and some of his personal belongings. In the entrance hall are the original plaster casts of some of his most famous pieces. In 1848, his tomb was moved to the museum's courtyard.

Folketinget

Formerly one of two elected chambers, this became Denmark's sole parliamentary body in 1953. You can attend the parliamentary debates at the public gallery of the main chamber, where its 179 elected members have a seat. At the right side in the front of the hall is the rostrum, from where members make their speeches during debates. However, during Question Time, they speak from their seats.

Castle Island

Several castles have stood on this site through the centuries. The first one was built in 1167 by Bishop Absalon. A second castle, occupied by the king, Eric of Pomerania, was built in 1417. When the building was beginning to fall apart, it was demolished in 1731 by Christian VI. In its place, he built a Baroque palace he considered suitable for an Absolute Monarch. It was completed in 1745, but was destroyed in the fire of 1794. Another castle was built in 1803–28, but also burned down in 1884. Finally, the present castle was built in 1907–28.

For full details and opening times for Teatermuseet and the Dansk Jødisk Museum, **see pp34–5.**

Detail from a painting showing the destruction of the Danish navy, 1801

Top 10 Moments in History

1 The Founding of Copenhagen

Copenhagen was founded around AD 1000 on the island of Slotsholmen *(see pp28–9)* by Sweyn I Forkbeard, son of Harald Bluetooth. Forkbeard was the first Danish king to strike coins with his image upon them. He subjugated Denmark, Norway and England, which he ruled for five weeks before his death in 1014.

2 The Growth of Trade

Given by Valdemar I to his adviser, Bishop Absalon, in the 1160s, the fishing village of Havn (harbour) prospered greatly from the shoals of herring that appeared in its waters. A castle was built here as protection against raiders. The prosperity of Havn became a threat to the Hanseatic league, an alliance of trading guilds that monopolized trade in Northern Europe. They repeatedly attacked the castle, finally destroying it in 1367.

3 Copenhagen, Capital of Denmark

King Erik VII took up residence in the second castle in 1416 and by this time Havn, now Kjøbmandehavn (Merchants' Harbour), was a major economic centre. It was proclaimed as the capital of Denmark in 1443.

Søren Kierkegaard

4 Civil War and the Reformation

Between 1534 and 1536, the Protestant king, Christian III successfully withstood an uprising against him in favour of his Catholic cousin, Christian II. Christian III brought about the Reformation in Denmark.

5 Absolute Monarchy

In 1660, Frederik III introduced Absolute Monarchy, enhancing the powers of the middle classes. Frederik VII later abolished it in favour of an elected Parliament.

6 Wars with Sweden

Sharing the Sound meant the Swedes and Danes were in constant dispute. In the winter of 1657, the Swedes crossed the frozen Sound on foot, attacking Copenhagen. The ensuing Treaty of Roskilde saw Denmark cede its Swedish territories.

Bombardment of Copenhagen, 1807

Preceding pages: Ceiling of the Marmorkirken dome.

Ceremony introducing Absolute Monarchy

The Great Plague

7 Between June 1711 and March 1712, Copenhagen was hit by bubonic plague, wiping out 20,000 of its 60,000 inhabitants. It is said to have been brought in by ships from Sweden or East Prussia, carrying infected vermin.

The Fire of 1728

8 In the month of October, within four days, the greatest fire in Copenhagen's history wiped out almost all of northern Copenhagen. It began early in the morning at Vester Kvarter 146 – now roughly at the top of Strøget. Five churches, the university library, and 1,600 houses were destroyed.

The Battles of Copenhagen

9 Early in the 19th century, the city suffered more lasting damage when the British attacked in 1801, destroying the Danish navy, and again in 1807 to discourage the Danes from supporting France in the Napoleonic wars.

Rescue of the Danish Jews

10 The Nazis occupied Denmark during World War II from 1940–45. In 1943, when the Jews were ordered to be deported to Germany, a collective of Danes and Swedes secretly evacuated by sea nearly the entire Jewish population to Sweden. As a result, most Danish Jews survived the war.

Top 10 Historical Figures

1 Harald Bluetooth (911–987)
He converted Denmark to Christianity.

2 King Cnut (994/5–1035)
Ruled England, Norway and Denmark for 20 years and famously failed to hold back the waves.

3 Bishop Absalon (1128–1201)
A warrior bishop, he built the first castle on Slotsholmen.

4 Christian IV (1577–1648)
He promoted shipping and trade and built the Rundetårn and Rosenborg Palace.

5 Tycho Brahe (1546–1601)
Brahe's astronomical tables were used to plot the rules of planetary motion.

6 Vitus Jonasson Bering (1681–1741)
A Danish explorer who discovered the Bering Strait, Sea, Island and Land Bridge.

7 Hans Christian Ørsted (1777–1851)
Danish physicist who discovered electromagnetism.

8 Søren Kierkegaard (1813–55)
A Danish philosopher, who first put forward the theory of "existentialism".

9 Knud Rasmussen (1879–1933)
He was the first man to cross the Northwest Passage by dogsled.

10 Niels Bohr (1885–1962)
A Nobel prize-winner (1922), he contributed vastly to the understanding of quantum mechanics.

Share your travel recommendations on traveldk.com

Left **Teatermuseet** Centre **Kunstindustrimuseet** Right **Thorvaldsens Museum**

Museums and Galleries

1 Ny Carlsberg Glyptotek

The museum houses a fabulous collection of antiquities from Egypt, Greece, Rome and the Mediterranean coast. You will also find an impressive collection of 19th- and early 20th-century Danish and French fine arts, including Impressionist and Post-Impressionist collections *(see pp24–5)*.

Egyptian statues at Ny Carlsberg Glyptotek

2 Nationalmuseet

This is Denmark's largest museum of cultural history. Here you can explore the history of the Danes right up to the present day. Artifacts range from Iron Age burials and Renaissance interiors to African masks and houses on stilts. Check out the museum's spectacular ethno-graphic collection including the world's oldest painting by South American Indians *(see pp26–7)*.

Viking culture at the Nationalmuseet

3 Statens Museum for Kunst

Nestled in a pretty park with lakes and grassy slopes, the National Gallery displays a large collection of inter-national art, including works by Great Masters like Dürer and Titian and by modern icons like Picasso and Matisse. It also showcases brilliant Danish collections that include work from the Skagen and modern schools *(see pp22–3)*.

4 Dansk Jødisk Museum

The Danish Jewish Museum tells the story of Denmark's Jewish community since the arrival of the first families in the 17th century. Designed by architect Daniel Libeskind, the interlocking interior symbolises Danish-Jewish good relations, its apogee the rescue of 7,000 Jews from Nazis. ◎ Map K5 • Proviant-passangen 6 • 33 11 22 18 • Open Sep–May 1pm–4pm Tue–Fri, noon–5pm Sat–Sun; Jun–Aug 10am–5pm Tue–Sun • Adm for adults; free with Copenhagen Card • www.jewmus.dk

5 Davids Samling

Set inside a 19th-century town house, the museum holds the collections of Christian Ludwig David (1878–1960), a Danish barrister. It includes fabulous furniture from the 18th–20th centuries and ancient Islamic ornamental art *(see p76)*.

For more museums and galleries, see pp19, 28–9, 56–7, 64–6, 78, 82–5, 90.

6 Teatermuseet
On display are sections including the stage, the auditorium and dressing rooms of the 18th-century Royal Theatre *(see p19)* that survived the fire of 1794.
® Map J5 • Christiansborg Ridebane 18 • 33 11 51 76 • Open 11am–3pm Tue & Thu, 11am–5pm Wed, 1pm–4pm Sat–Sun • Adm for adults; free with Copenhagen Card • www.teatermuseet.dk

7 Frihedsmuseet
The Danish Resistance Museum is part of the national collection. It takes you through a fascinating exploration of Danish life during the Nazi occupation from 1940–45 *(see p77)*.

8 Kunstindustrimuseet
One half of the Danish Museum of Decorative Art holds a collection of Chinese and Japanese artifacts, as well as European medieval and Rococo arts. The other half is dedicated to cutting-edge Danish 20th- and 21st-century design. English labelling is limited. *(see p77)*.

9 Thorvaldsens Museum
Opened in 1848, this museum pays homage to the Neo-Classical sculptor, Bertel Thorvaldsen. It includes most of his works, as well as some private belongings. You can also visit his grave, transferred here from Vor Frue Kirke in 1848, four years after his demise *(see p28)*.

10 Den Hirschsprungske Samling
Housed in a villa, across the lake from the Statens Museum for Kunst, it features a collection of late 19th- and early 20th-century Danish art – notably the Skagen school, Denmark's equally appealing answer to the Impressionists *(see p75)*.

Top 10 Danish Artists

1 Bertel Thorvaldsen (1770–1844)
Son of an Icelandic wood carver, he became Denmark's most famous sculptor.

2 Christoffer Eckersberg (1783–1853)
Laid the foundations for the "Golden Age of Painting" in Denmark (1800–1850).

3 Michael Ancher (1849–1927)
One of the best-known artists in Denmark and the unofficial head of the Skagen group.

4 Peder Severin Krøyer (1851–1909)
His work is inspired by the lives of the fishermen of Skagen.

5 Anna Ancher (1859–1935)
A Skagen artist and wife of Michael Ancher. Her work is typified by picturesque, intimate scenes of family life.

6 Vilhelm Hammershøi (1864–1916)
Known for his paintings of interiors, done in muted colours.

7 Henry Heerup (1907–1993)
Joined the CoBrA group in 1949. His work is fantastical and sometimes humorous with a touch of melancholy.

8 Richard Mortensen (1910–1993)
The first Danish artist to turn to abstraction. Also known for his perfect technical finish.

9 Carl-Henning Pedersen (1913–2007)
An expressionist surrealist and one of the most influential artists of the CoBrA group.

10 Asger Jorn (1914–73)
Founder of CoBrA, an important art group to emerge after World War II.

For museums and galleries out of town, see pp96–102.

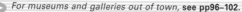

Left **Rosenborg Slot** Centre **Den Sorte Diamant** Right **Christiansborg Slot**

🔟 Historic Buildings

Rosenborg Slot

1 This lovely, turreted Renaissance castle was built by Christian IV. Now a royal museum, its collections and interior provide a vivid picture of the monarchy over the centuries. The crown jewels are on display in the basement *(see pp14–15)*.

Chapel Portal at Frederiksborg Slot

Christiansborg Slot

2 This Neo-Baroque palace, built in the early 20th century, is the seat of the government and the fourth palace on the site. Visit the 11th–14th-century ruins of the first two castles built here, the 18th-century theatre and stables and the state rooms *(see p28)*.

Rundetårn

3 This curious tower-like building, built by Christian IV, affords a wonderful view over the old town. It also has a gallery that holds innovative, changing exhibitions *(see p16)*.

Børsen

4 The stock exchange is remarkable for its tower with a striking spire designed to look like four entwined dragons' tails. The three crowns at the top of the building represent the kingdoms of Denmark, Sweden and Norway. 🇩🇰 *Map K5 • Børsgade • Not open to the public*

Frederiksborg Slot

5 This beautiful, grand Renaissance castle is a short train ride away from Copenhagen. Christian IV was living here when he fell seriously ill and demanded to be taken to his favourite palace, Rosenborg, for his last few days. Don't miss the castle's ornate chapel *(see p98)*.

Regensen

6 Built by Christian IV in the 17th century as a student hostel, Regensen still retains that function today. Unfortunately, most of the building was burnt down in the city fire of 1728 *(see p33)*, but so vital was it to the life of the university that it was rebuilt in the same year *(see p17)*.

SAS Radisson Royal Hotel

7 A 1960s icon or a horrible tower block? Designed by architect Arne Jacobsen *(see p39)*, this hotel underwent a makeover in the 1980s; the original interior was retained only in Room 606. If it is unoccupied and you ask nicely, they might let you have a look at the room. The foyer has a 1960s retro cool look and includes Jacobsen's interesting Swan and Egg chairs. You can enjoy excellent views of the city from the restaurant *(see also p83)*.

 For more historic churches, see pp40–41.

Holmen's Kirke

8 The only Renaissance church in Copenhagen, it was originally built as a sailors' forge in 1562–63 and converted into a naval church by Christian IV in 1619. The strangely exotic font is the work of a local 17th-century blacksmith. The metal fence shows golden elephants carrying black castles on their backs, a depiction of the royal Danish elephant. ⚓ *Map K5 • Holmens Kanal • 33 13 61 78 • Open 9am–2pm Mon–Sat*

Den Sorte Diamant

9 The Black Diamond, a modern extension of the Royal Library, was built by architects Schmidt, Hammer and Lassen. It has the National Museum of Photography, the Queen's Hall concert space and an exhibition area. The shiny tiled exterior is highly reflective and a favourite photo opportunity for the boat trippers floating past *(see p8)*.

Operaen

10 Opened in January 2005, the Opera House stands on the banks of the Holmen, formerly Copenhagen's naval dockyard. The auditorium is a masterpiece of acoustic design, from the velour seats that do not absorb sound, to the distance between the front of the stage and the back wall, which allows for the perfect time to achieve greater clarity for opera. Over 100,000 pieces of 23.75 carat gold leaves make up the ceiling *(see p8)*.

Operaen

Top 10 Statues

Little Mermaid

1 The city's icon, inspired by the fairy tale. ⚓ *Langelinie, top end of Kastellet*

Gefionspringvandet

2 Statue depicting the fable of goddess Gefion and the king of Denmark. ⚓ *Langelinie, by St Alban's Church*

Fiskerkone

3 The Fishwife was created in 1940 and installed at the spot where fish have been sold since the medieval times. ⚓ *Gammel Strand*

Lurblæserne

4 It is said that the Hornblowers will sound the Viking horns whenever a virgin passes by – no one has heard a peep out of them yet. ⚓ *Rådhuspladsen*

Frederik V

5 Sculptor Jacques Saly took 20 years to finish this statue. Unveiled in 1771, it merited a 27-gun salute. ⚓ *Amalienborg Slotsplads*

Christian V

6 Shows the king dressed as a Roman emperor riding over a fallen figure. ⚓ *Kongens Nytorv*

Hans Christian Andersen

7 Famous sculpture by Henry Lukow-Nielsen. ⚓ *Corner of Rådhus, HC Andersen Boulevard*

Hans Christian Andersen

8 Includes scenes from his fairy tales. ⚓ *Kongens Have*

Caritasspringvandet

9 One of the oldest statues in Copenhagen dating back to 1608. ⚓ *Gammel Torv*

The Elephant Gateway

10 Big, splendid elephants at the Carlsberg Brewery gateway. ⚓ *Gammel Carlsberg Vej 11*

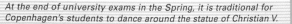

At the end of university exams in the Spring, it is traditional for Copenhagen's students to dance around the statue of Christian V.

Left **Vor Frue Kirke** Centre **Hotel d'Angleterre** Right **Nyhavn**

Hans Christian Andersen Sights

1 Det Kongelige Teater
Hans Christian Andersen arrived in Copenhagen on 6 September 1819 as a starstruck 14-year-old. It was "my second birthday", he recounts in his biography, *The Fairytale of My Life*. Determined to become an actor, he went straight to the Royal Theatre in search of a job. Although occasionally employed as an actor, his acting talent never quite matched his skill as a writer *(see p18)*.

2 Bakkehusmuseet
The Bakkehus (House on the Hill) was the home of prominent literary patron Knud Rahbek and his wife Kamma Lyhne Rahbek from 1802–1830. Andersen met the couple in the early 1820s and their home soon became a meeting place for poets and authors. The museum retains a homely atmosphere and recreates the Golden Age of creativity. It also includes mementos that belonged to Andersen *(see pp84–5)*.

3 Vingårdsstræde 6
Andersen lived here for a year in 1827 in a spartan garret room (then No 132), preparing for his university exams. This is where he wrote the sad poem, *The Student*. The museum's entrance is on the third floor of the Magasin du Nord *(see p19)*.

4 Nyhavn Nos 20, 67 and 18
Andersen lived in lodgings in Nyhavn for much of his life, including at Nyhavn 280 (now No 20) in 1834, No 67 in 1848 and No 18 (a private hotel) in 1871. He lived here until 1875, when he fell terminally ill and moved in with the Melchiors, who nursed him in their own home *(see p18)*.

5 Magasin du Nord
In 1838, Andersen moved into Hotel du Nord, now the department store Magasin du Nord. Here he rented two rooms in the attic, one of which overlooked the Royal Theatre. Mini's Café (now Café à Porta) was next door and became a regular haunt for the writer *(see p18)*.

6 Rundetårn
The exhibition space here was once the university library where Andersen spent many hours. His first fairytale, *The Tinderbox* (1835), talks of a dog with eyes "as big as a tower" guarding a

Department store, Magasin (once Hotel) du Nord

For more on HC Andersen, see the Wonderful World of HC Andersen Museum on **pp56**, **66** and the Bakkehusmuseet on **p84**.

Rundetårn's cobbled spiral ramp

treasure. Scholars believe this refers to the Rundetårn, which was built as an observatory – a literal eye to the sky *(see p16)*.

Hotel d'Angleterre
Andersen stayed here in November 1860, when he occupied two rooms at the corner of Kongens Nytorv and Østergade (Strøget), close to the Royal Theatre; between August 1869 and March 1870; and finally, during April–May 1871 *(see p112)*.

Lille Kongensgade 1
In October 1866, Andersen took a suite of rooms on the third floor, rented out by a photographer, Thora Hallager. Here, he bought furniture for the first time in his life (at the age of 61), as this was an unfurnished apartment. ◈ *Map K4*

Vor Frue Kirke
Andersen died on 4 August 1875 of liver cancer. His funeral, a national event attended by the king and crown prince, was held at Vor Frue Kirke in the Old Town *(see p17)*.

Assistens Kirkegård
This is the cemetery where Andersen's body was interred in Nørrebro. The stone is inscribed with inspirational lines from his poem "Oldingen" or "The Old Man" (1874) *(see p75)*.

Top 10 Cultural Figures

1 August Bournonville (1805–1879)
Choreographer and ballet master who created many works for the Danish ballet.

2 Carl Nielsen (1865–1931)
Composer, violinist and pianist. Best known for his symphonies and the operas *Saul og David* and *Maskerade*.

3 Karen Blixen (1885–1962)
Her famous novel, *Out of Africa (1937)*, was published under the pen name Isak Dinesen.

4 Poul Henningsen (1894–1967)
Architect, author and anti-traditionalist. Best known for his PH lamps *(see p47)*.

5 Arne Jacobsen (1902–1971)
Architect and designer who defined the concept of Danish design – fluid and practical.

6 Lars von Trier (1956–)
Film director famous for the Dogme95 Collective and his technique of cinematic minimalism.

7 Peter Høeg (1957–)
Gained international acclaim for his story *Miss Smilla's Feeling for Snow* (1992).

8 Viggo Mortensen (1958–)
Popular as Aragorn in *The Lord of the Rings* films.

9 Helena Christensen (1968–)
Miss Denmark (1986) and a Super Model of the 1990s.

10 Thomas Vinterberg (1969–)
Screenwriter, director and co-founder of Dogme95.

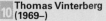

Left **Christians Kirke** Right **Marmorkirken** Right **Sankt Petri Kirke**

Churches

Helligåndskirken
Dating back to the 12th century, these are among the oldest architectural remains in Copenhagen. Only Helligånds-huset (now used for markets and exhibitions), Christian IV's Baroque portal and Griffenfeld's Chapel survive. Much of the original church burnt down in the fire of 1728. The church re-opened after reconstruction in 1732 *(see p16)*.

Christians Kirke
This church was built in the Rococo style in 1755–59 by Nicolai Eigtved, Frederik V's master architect. It is starkly different from most Danish churches: instead of the congregation sitting only in pews in the nave, the church has a second gallery level (like that of a theatre) where all the important worshippers are seated *(see p89)*.

Vor Frelsers Kirke
This splendid Baroque church was built in 1682–96 at the behest of Christian V. The king's royal insignia can be seen at various places in the church, including on the organ case that is supported by elephants, the symbol of Denmark's prestigious Order of the Elephant. The spire is 90 m (295 ft) high, and the tower affords a magnificent view of the city. The interior of the church is bright and well-lit, thanks to the white walls and tall windows *(see p89)*.

Trinitatis Kirke
Standing next door to the Rundetårn is the Trinitatis Kirke. Commissioned by Christian IV in 1637, this lovely church was completed in the reign of Frederik III in 1656. The present interior dates back to 1731, as the original was burnt in the fire of 1728. It includes boxed pews with seashell carvings, a gilded altarpiece, a Baroque dark wood pulpit and a fabulous gold and silver coloured organ *(see p16)*.

Vor Frue Kirke
Also known as St Mary's Cathedral, the church has been on this site in different forms since the 12th century and has played host to royal and national events over the years. The church has a 19th-century façade and a bright interior dominated by statues of Christ and his Apostles *(see p16)*.

Holmens Kirke

6 Sankt Petri Kirke

This is the city's oldest church. Unlike most medieval buildings, it survived the fire of 1728. Its tower, nave and choir date back to the 15th century. The north and south transepts were added in 1634 *(see p16)*.

7 Holmens Kirke

Originally built in 1562 as a naval forge, it was converted into a church in 1619. The Baroque altarpiece is fantastically ornate, and the pulpit is the tallest in Denmark *(see p37)*.

8 Marmorkirken

This circular church has an imposing presence. The dome's interior is covered with paintings of the 12 Apostles and light floods in from 12 skylights. Originally designed by Nicolai Eigtved in 1740, work on the building was suspended in 1770 due to increasing expenses and began again after nearly 150 years, financed by Carl Frederik Tietgen and redesigned by Ferdinand Meldahl. It was finally inaugurated on 19 August 1894 *(see p20)*.

9 Grundtvigs Kirke

This suburban parish church was built in the 1920s–30s by PV Jensen Klint and his son. It has yellow-brick walls and an impressive modern Gothic appearance. To visit take the train to Emdrup. ✦ *På Bjerget 14B, Bispebjerg • 35 81 54 42 • Open 9am–4pm Mon–Wed, Fri & Sat; 9am–6pm Thu; May–Sep 12pm–4pm Sun; Oct–Apr 12pm–1pm Sun.*

Grundtvigs Kirke

10 Christiansborg Slotskirke

The original 18th-century Rococo creation was destroyed in the palace fire of 1794 and was rebuilt in a Neo-Classical style with a central dome. Inaugurated on Whit Sunday in 1826 to mark the 1,000th anniversary of Christianity in Denmark, it succumbed to another fire in 1992, but has now been rebuilt *(see p28)*.

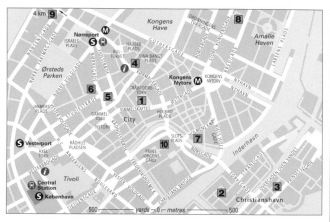

Further afield, don't miss Roskilde's Gothic brick cathedral which doubles as a mausoleum for the Danish Royal Family, **see p100.**

Left **Det Kongelige Teater** Right **Copenhagen Jazz House**

Performing Art and Music Venues

Operaen

1 Operaen
Famed for its acoustics, the Opera House attracts a variety of international productions. You can enjoy a good view of the stage from any seat and all the seats are relatively cheap due to government subsidy *(see p8)*.

2 Det Kongelige Teater
This is a great destination for a night of entertainment. World-class performances of ballet and drama are held at the old stage or the Stærekøssen which is next door to the main theatre building *(see p18)*.

3 Copenhagen Jazz House
Here you can enjoy all kinds of modern jazz – from classic and vocal to electronic, Neo-Bebop and Latin rhythms. There is a bar and a large dance floor as well. Keep an eye out for celebrities. ✆ *Map J4 • Niels Hemmingsensgade 10 • 33 15 26 00 • www.jazzhouse.dk*

4 Mojo Bluesbar
Smoky, small, dark and intimate, this bar is known for its laidback blues and live jazz performances. There won't be any distracting gimmicks or performance technology on display here. It is very popular, so book ahead. ✆ *Map H5 •Løngangstræde 21C • 33 11 64 53; Booking: 23 44 97 77 • www.mojo.dk*

5 Wallmans Saloner
This circular former circus building (1884) is now a glamorous venue offering old-fashioned "dinner, show and dancing". There is surround-entertainment on seven stages while resting members of the cast servo you a good dinner. After the show, it turns into a nightclub. ✆ *Map G5 • Cirkusbyningen, Jernbanegade 8 • 33 16 37 00 • www.wallmans.dk*

6 Tivoli Koncertsal
The Tivoli Concert Hall is the city's largest music venue, with a capacity of 1,900. It stages over 100 operas, ballets, rock and jazz concerts during the Tivoli season *(see p11)*.

Mojo Bluesbar

Tivoli Koncertsal

Top 10 Jazz Venues and Events

1 Bars and Cafés
Popular places include Dan Turèll (www.danturell.dk), Kaffesalonen *(see p79)* and Thorvaldsens Hus *(see p67)*.

2 Pumpehuset
Music venue in the Latin Quarter seating 600. ◎ *Studiestræde 52 • 33 93 19 60 • www.pumpehuset.dk*

3 Slotsholmen
Look out for shows at different venues *(see pp28–9)*.

4 Pressen
Formerly a printing press, now a prime venue for the Jazz Festival. ◎ *Politikens Hus, Rådhuspladsen 37 • 33 93 20 13*

5 Huset
Specializes in traditional jazz and swing. ◎ *Rådhusstræde 13 • 33 69 32 00*

6 Zum Biergarten
Dedicated to a series called Urban Jazz Visits. ◎ *Axeltorv 12 • 33 93 90 94*

7 M/S Stubnitz
A 1964 steel ferry hosting concerts and parties throughout the Jazz Festival. ◎ *Next to Langebro bridge, Christians Brygge 9 • 28 78 41 98*

8 Havnescenen
Harbour setting with grilled food and a "jazz on the water" experience. ◎ *Islands Brygge 18 • 32 95 13 94*

9 La Fontaine
Among the more grittier venues. Late night jazz Tue–Sat. ◎ *Kompagnistræde 11 • 33 11 60 98*

10 Open Air Venues
Check out Tivoli, Kongens Nytorv, Islands Brygge, Kongens Have, Gråbrødre Torv, Blågårds Plads and Israels Plads. ◎ *www.jazzfestival.dk*

7 Det Ny Teater
This early 20th-century theatre hosts popular international musicals, such as *Phantom of the Opera* and *The Producers*. ◎ *Map C5 • Gammel Kongevej 29 • 33 25 50 75 • www.detnyteater.dk*

8 Koncerthuset
Designed by architect Jean Nouvel, this concert hall is shaped like a meteorite, inspired by the Danish novel *Miss Smilla's Feeling for Snow*. It is due to open in early 2009 as part of the new development area in Ørestad. ◎ *Emil Holms Kanal 20 • 35 20 30 40 • www.dr.dk/koncerthuset*

9 Parken
This football stadium held its first indoor concert in 2001 with the Eurovision Song Concert. Famous bands like U2, Metallica and The Black Eyed Peas have performed here since. ◎ *Map D2*

10 Loppen
This is the best indie rock venue in town. Bands like Franz Ferdinand, Interpol and Antony & the Johnsons performed here long before they hit the big time. ◎ *Map M5 • Bådsmandsstræde 43, Christianshavn • 32 57 84 22 • Open 9pm–late • www.loppen.dk*

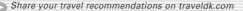

Left **A brunch café at Halmtorvet** Right **Cyclists relaxing at Rosenborg Slot**

Outdoor Activities

A harbour trip

Bikes
Almost every major road in Copenhagen has a cycle lane and you can hire a bike *(see p106)* for a day or more. In summer, you can hop onto a free City Bike (provided for a refundable fee by the city of Copenhagen across 125 City Bike Parking places) and ride within city limits.

Harbour Trips
Harbour trips are a lovely way to see the city. There are two canal tour companies *(see p7)*; both begin trips at Nyhavn. You can also tour the city on a harbour bus. If you are carrying a Copenhagen Card *(see p111)*, you can change buses using just a single ticket.

Outdoor Dining
In the 1990s, Copenhagen witnessed a surge in outdoor dining venues. Now, virtually all cafés and restaurants offer outdoor dining in the summer. Blankets and heaters are provided for when it gets chilly. Nyhavn and Peblinge Dossering offer particularly good views.

Flea Markets
There are many outdoor flea markets in the summer, offering everything from furniture and clothing to pseudo-antiques and retro vinyl. ◉ *Frederiksberg Rådhusplads: Map A5; 8am–3pm Sat • Gammel Strand: Map J4; 8am–5pm Fri–Sat • Israel Plads: Map H3; 8am–3pm Sat*
- *Kongens Nytorv: Map K4; 9am–5pm Sat*
- *Nørrebrogade: Map C3; 10am–4pm Sat*

Tivoli
At Tivoli, you can wander through the stalls, check out the rides, listen to the Tivoli bands (free rock and pop concerts on Friday nights), or simply relax on a lakeside bench *(see pp10–11)*.

Lounging by the Reservoirs
Water reservoirs divide the main city from Nørrebro and Østerbro.

Flea market at Gammel Strand

Zoologisk Have

Of these, Skt Jørgens Sø, Peblinge Sø and Sortedam Sø are easily accessible. You can lounge along their grassy banks or enjoy the scenic view from the bridges that cross them.

7 Dyrehaven

This deer park (it does still have lots of deer – the rutting season is in the autumn), has been here since the 16th century. It is like an English park or common and features a noisy, enjoyable fun fair. For a bit of excitement, take a pony and trap ride. ◈ Map B2 • Dyrehaven Klampenborg • www.bakken.dk

8 Kongens Have

Attached to Rosenborg Slot, the King's Garden is a great place to sunbathe, play frisbee, cricket, football or have a picnic. In the summer, you can catch a puppet show or a jazz concert (see pp14–15).

9 Assistens Kirkegård

This beautiful, meandering churchyard holds the graves of famous Danes like HC Andersen, August Bournonville and Niels Bohr (see p75).

10 Zoologisk Have

You will find polar bears, lions, tigers, elephants and other animals in this delightful zoo. There are thematic adventure trails for kids (see p83).

Top 10 Beaches and Pools

1 Havnebadet
Popular floating harbour pool with fresh water. ◈ Islands Brygge • 23 71 31 89

2 Bellevue
Full of people playing, sailing or relaxing. Left end is nudist. ◈ Strandvejen 340, 2930 Klampenborg

3 Fælledparkens Soppesø
Huge, child-friendly outdoor pool with an ice-cream kiosk. ◈ Borgmester Jensens Allé 50, Østerbro • 35 39 08 04

4 Amager Strandpark
Luxury beach with a huge lagoon, pool and snack kiosks. ◈ Amager Strandvej, 2300 Copenhagen • 33 66 35 00 • www.amager-strand.dk

5 Køge Bugt Strandpark
Several beautiful beaches along Køge Bay. ◈ Ishøj Store Torv 20, 2635 Ishøj

6 Bellahøj Friluftsbad
The city's largest open-air swimming facility. ◈ Bellahøjvej 1, Brønshøj • 38 60 16 66

7 Frederiksdal Fribad
Gorgeous lakeside beach. ◈ Frederiksdal Badesti 1, Virum • 45 83 81 85

8 DGI-Byen
Includes a "super-ellipse" pool, kids' pool and a spa pool. ◈ Corner of Tietgensgade and Ingerslevsgade • 33 29 80 00

9 Charlottenlund Beach
Good place for sunbathing. ◈ Park Strandvejen 144, Charlottenlund

10 Frederiksberg Svømmehal
Includes a kids' pool, solarium, massage services, steam rooms and wood saunas. ◈ Helgesvej 29, 2000 Frederiksberg • 38 14 04 04

 For more outdoor activities beyond Copenhagen, see pp96–102.

Left **Girlie Hurley Shop** Centre **Shopping street, Strøget (north)** Right **Shop front, Bredgade**

🔟 Shopping Districts

1 Strøget
This is Copenhagen's equivalent of London's Oxford Street. The shops, which stretch across five linked pedestrian streets, range from cheerful and inexpensive outlets to designer and upmarket department stores (towards Kongens Nytorv). It has something for everyone, from bargain clothes to exclusive silver, porcelain and glassware of the Royal Scandinavia shops. Strøget is also popular for its street performers (see p66).

2 Off Strøget (North)
Heading up north from Strøget, you will find numerous little boutiques, record stores and secondhand shops. Indulge in some individual shopping at streets like Skindergade, Larsbjørnstræde, Vestergade, Studiestræde and Sankt Peders Stræde. ◎ Map H4–J4

Strøget

Glam clothes shop at Nørrebro

3 Off Strøget (South)
The streets to the south of Strøget are great for "alternative" shopping. Læderstræde and Kompagnistræde are especially good, the latter mostly for its antique shops. ◎ Map J4–J5

4 Kronprinsensgade
This posh shopping area includes many of Scandinavia's top designer brands, such as Stig P and Bruuns Bazaar. You will also find Scandinavia's oldest tea shop, Perch's Tea Room. ◎ Map J4

5 Nansensgade
Located on the outskirts of the old town, this area has a mix of traditional and trendy boutiques, as well as good restaurants and cafés. ◎ Map G3

6 Nørrebro
This cool and trendy area is filled with secondhand stores and chic boutiques offering street youth fashion. Check out the shops to the east of the Assistens Cemetery around Sankt Hans Torv. ◎ Map D3

For more shopping alternatives, see pp80, 86, 92.

7 Vesterbro

This former red light area is now a gritty shopping district offering good bargains. Among the more interesting streets are Istedgade, which is lined with boutiques and art shops and Værnedamsvej, which has several independent fashion stores and gourmet food shops. ⊗ *Map C5–C6*

8 Frederiksberg

Along Gammel Kongevej, Frederiksberg's main thoroughfare, you will find excellent shops catering to affluent tastes with prices to match. ⊗ *Map B5*

9 Fisketorv Shopping Centre

Situated on the waterfront facing the Inner Harbour, this city mall is a few minutes away from the Copencabana harbour pool. It has over 120 shops, several restaurants and a multiplex cinema. ⊗ *Map J6 • Kalvebod Brygge 59, Vesterbro • 35 37 19 17 • Open 10am–8pm Mon–Fri, 10am–5pm Sat, first Sunday of the month*

10 Bredgade

If you are looking for traditional, pre-20th-century antiques, this is the perfect place to visit. Here you will find several grand-looking shops and auction houses that sell all kinds of antiques, including authentic paintings and statues. ⊗ *Map L3*

Kronprinsensgade

Top 10 Danish Design Companies

1 Holmegaard Glass
Danish glass company. Products are hand-blown. ⊗ *Holmegaard Glasværk, Glasværksvej 54, Fensmark, DK-4684 Holmegaard • 55 54 50 00 • Adm • www.holmegaard.com*

2 Cylinda-Line (by Arne Jacobsen)
Popular tableware collection (1967). Combines steel, wood and plastic.

3 Bang & Olufsen
Known for their cutting-edge audio-visual designs. ⊗ *www.bang-olufsen.com*

4 Kaare Klint Furniture
Combines ergonomics with elegant 18th-century English styles.

5 Bodum
Classic and smart kitchenware in steel and glass. ⊗ *www.bodum.com*

6 Lego
These popular building blocks were introduced in 1952. ⊗ *www.lego.com*

7 Pins Stool
A contemporary stool design (2002) by the furniture designer, Hans Sandgren Jacobsen.

8 Flora Danica Porcelain
Royal porcelain design featuring floral motifs. ⊗ *www.royalcopenhagen.com*

9 Poul Henningsen Lamps
Famous lamp design, creating the effect of maximum light and minimum shadow. ⊗ *www.poul-henningsen.com*

10 Georg Jensen Silverware
Original, organic tableware designs and casual jewellery. ⊗ *www.jensensilver.com*

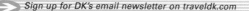

Left **Formel B** Right **Le Sommelier**

Restaurants

Ensemble
This sophisticated restaurant impresses with its cool, clean lines, minimalist lighting, mushroom-coloured walls and crisp linen-draped tables. The regularly changing fixed price menu with accompanying wines offers six courses of beautifully arranged cuisine. Map K4
• Tordenskjoldsgade 11 • 33 11 33 52
• Open 6pm–10pm Tue–Sat • www.restaurantensemble.dk • ⓚⓚⓚⓚⓚ

Umami
While the slick, contemporary design and attentive service here are noteworthy, it is the food that really stands out. The delicate flavours that arise from combining Japanese and French cuisines have to be experienced to be believed. Map K3 • Store Kongensgade 59 • 33 38 75 00 • Open 6–10pm Sun–Thu, 6–11pm Fri–Sat
• www.restaurantumami.dk • ⓚⓚⓚⓚⓚ

Kong Hans Kælder
This restaurant has white-washed, underlit arches in Copenhagen's oldest building. Watch the chef in the open kitchen as he cooks up fancy dishes from the à la carte and fixed price menus. Map K4
• Vingårdsstræde 6 • 33 32 62 63
• Open 6pm–midnight Mon–Sat • www.konghans.dk • ⓚⓚⓚⓚⓚ

Kokkeriet
Enjoy relaxed modern dining in the brightly lit, single room overlooking Nyboder. Share in the dining experience with only a few fellow diners (nine tables and a private dining room) and enjoy the six-course menu, or choose from the quality changing menu. Map K2
• Kronprinsessegade 64 • 33 15 27 77
• Open 6pm–1am Tue–Sat • www.kokkeriet.dk • ⓚⓚⓚⓚⓚ

Era Ora
Umbrian cuisine is served in this well-established Italian restaurant. Enjoy lunchtime al fresco dining or fuller evening menus (of 12–17 small dishes) in this 18th-century building's warmly decorated room. Several combined food and wine lists are also available up to 3,800kr (see p93).

Frikadeller

Godt
The modest blue-painted exterior conceals a fabulous dining experience at this appropriately named ("good") restaurant. The English chef regularly wanders amongst the 20-seater restaurant adding that personal touch to this husband-wife enterprise.
Map K3 • Gothersgade 38 • 33 15 21 22 • Open 6pm–midnight Tue–Sat
• ⓚⓚⓚⓚⓚ

For more restaurants and a key to price categories, **see pp67, 71, 79, 87, 93, 103.**

7 Noma
Voted among the world's top ten restaurants by *Restaurant* magazine, Noma offers superior Nordic fare sourced from Denmark, Iceland, Greenland and the Faroe Islands. Run by chef René Redzepi, the restaurant is housed in a fabulous warehouse dating from 1767. The interior has a northern shabby chic look with open beams. It is Denmark's only 2-star restaurant to have been featured in the new Michelin Guide *(see p93)*.

8 Le Sommelier
A first-rate French restaurant, with impeccable staff, a pleasant atmosphere and a massive wine list. The foie gras is delicious. In the right season, be sure to try the seafood. The chocolate plate laden with five different chocolate-inspired confections is hard to resist. ⊗ *Map L3 • Bredgade 63–65 • 33 11 45 15 • Open noon–2pm & 6–10pm Mon–Thu, noon–2pm & 6–11pm Fri, 6–11pm Sat, 6–10pm Sun • www.lesommelier.dk • ⊛⊛⊛⊛*

9 Formel B
Beautifully prepared, French-style cuisine using fresh Danish ingredients is the key to the tasty dishes served in this charming restaurant. Winter fare includes raw marinated shrimps with squid and soy-ginger browned butter *(see p87)*.

10 Meet the Danes
If you fancy some good, traditional Danish home cooking and want to see how the locals live, Meet the Danes is an organization that gives you the opportunity to do just that. A must-stop for groups and independent travellers. ⊗ *Map G4–H5 • Vester Voldgade 85 • 23 28 43 47 • www.meetthedanes.dk*

Top 10 Danish dishes

1 Frikadeller
Pork and veal meatballs, fried in butter and usually served with potatoes.

2 Stegt Flæsk
A classic Danish dish. Fried slices of pork on the bone with a creamy parsley sauce and potatoes.

3 Smørrebrødsmad
An open sandwich usually made with rye bread. Beef with horseradish sauce is a popular topping.

4 Skipperlabskovs
Beef, marinated for 24 hours in brine and stewed with potatoes, bay leaves and black peppercorns.

5 Sol Over Gudhjem
A typical Bornholm dish. Smoked herring, topped with egg yolk, onion and chives.

6 Marinerede Sild
Herring, marinated in vinegar and spices, served with onion and capers. Tastes best with rye bread.

7 Rødkål
A common way of cooking Rødkål (red cabbage) is stewing it for 40 minutes with apples, vinegar and sugar.

8 Kogt Hamburgerryg
A Danish staple of pork loin cooked with thyme and parsley, accompanied by boiled potatoes, vegetables; horseradish or mustard sauce is often added for taste.

9 Ris à l'Amande
Rice pudding with almonds, served cold and topped with warm cherry sauce. A popular Christmas-time dessert.

10 Gulerodskage
Carrot cake made with walnuts and often served with whipped cream.

Left **Thé à la Menthe** Right **Emmerys Bakery**

Cafés and Bars

Laundromat Café

Bastionen and Løven
Set inside an old mill in Christianshavn, this is one of the most romantic eateries in Copenhagen. It is famous for its weekend brunches, so try to get there early *(see p93)*.

Laundromat Café
There is a lot you can do at this cheerful, "hybrid" café. You can pop your laundry into one of the Laundromat machines and relax with a cup of coffee, or have lunch. You can also browse through the newspapers and second-hand books on offer.
◈ *Map C3* • *Elmegade 15, Nørrebro*
• *35 35 26 72*

Emmerys Bakery
This is Denmark's foremost organic gourmet store. Primarily a bakery, it is also known to sell sandwiches, drinks and an array of beautifully packaged gourmet food. It has a nice café area where you can sample their goods, anytime from breakfast onwards *(see p86)*.

Rabes Have
This 17th-century pub has a tasteful decor, with dark green and white walls and a pretty garden at the back. The food served here is mostly organic and traditional open sandwiches are offered at lunchtime. In the summer months, it also provides catering services to Kunstindustrimuseet *(see p93)*.

Pussy Galore's Flying Circus
This is one of the first cafés to have opened in trendy Nørrebro. They serve good food and in the summer, you can sit out on the cobbled square and enjoy your snack *(see p79)*.

Kontiki Bar
This refreshing bar is set on a boat, just behind the Opera House on Holmen. Located far from the bustle of busy tourist areas, you can sit out on the deck for drinks and snacks, or have a more formal meal in the cabin. It is advisable to book ahead. ◈ *Map M4* • *Takkelloftvej 1Z* • *29 46 54 17* • *www.kontikibar.dk*

Bådteatret
Located on the south side of Nyhavn, the Bådteatret, or Theatre Boat, offers drinks and snacks at reasonable prices and affords good views of the harbour. If you are well-versed with Danish, be sure to

Pussy Galore's Flying Circus

catch one of the experimental theatre performances that take place in the hold. Ⓢ *Map L4*
• *Nyhavn*

8 Thé à la Menthe

This lovely little basement Moroccan tea salon offers great cold drinks, tea and meze. The decor is Moroccan, with kilms and water-pipes. Yet, it retains a Danish feel with cream-coloured wall panelling and pale green divans. If you like the decor, be sure to visit their shop on Rådhusstræde. Ⓢ *Map J5*
• *Kompagnistræde 29 • 33 33 00 38*
• *www.thealamenthe.dk*

9 Salonen

This wonderfully cosy café is a firm favourite with both international students and locals. The laid-back atmosphere makes Salonen a great place to lounge and relax with a large cup of coffee or tea. For those in need of greater sustenance, the friendly staff serve up hearty food from the fusion/crossover menu – prepared in a kitchen little bigger than a square metre. Ⓢ *Map H4 • Saint Peders Stræde 20*
• *33 11 21 11 • Open noon–midnight Mon–Wed, noon–1am Thu–Sun*

10 La Glace

Located just off Strøget, La Glace is one of the foremost (and the oldest) confectioneries in Copenhagen, offering mouth-watering cakes and chocolates. Both coffee and cakes are beautifully presented, and they are best savoured in the Old-World ambience created by the traditional polished-wood interiors. Ⓢ *Map H4 • Skoubogade 3–5 • 33 14 46 46 • Open 8:30am–5:30pm Mon–Thu, 8:30am–6pm Fri, 9am–5pm Sat, closed on Sun, except Sep–Easter Open 11am–5pm Sun*
• *www.laglace.dk*

The interior of La Glace

For more cafés and bars, see pp52–5, 79, 81 and 93.

A night out at the Culture Box

Nightlife Venues

Søpavillonen

1 Søpavillonen

Great tribute bands perform at this stunning lakeside pavilion, recently transformed into a restaurant, bar and spacious dance floor. DJs play a mix of 1970s and 1980s disco, with elements of Latin, rock and Danish pop.
⊗ Map C4 • Gyldenløvesgade 24 • 33 15 12 24 • Open 9pm–5am daily • Over 25 years only • www.soepavillonen.dk

2 Rust

Trendy Rust is at the cutting edge of the local music and clubbing scene. It showcases up-and-coming acts and top international DJs playing an eclectic mix of sounds. ⊗ Map C3
• Guldbergsgade 8 • 35 24 52 00 • Open 9pm–5am Wed–Sat • Nightclub: over 20 years only • www.rust.dk

3 Park Diskotek

This sophisticated venue plays an exciting range of music. There are several dance floors here. ⊗ Map E2• Østerbrogade 79
• 35 25 16 61 • Open 11pm–5am Fri–Sat, 11pm–4am Thu • Min age: 18 (Thu), 20 (Fri), 22 (Sat) • www.park.dk

4 The Rock

This club offers the total rock experience – from heavy metal and hard rock to rock'n'roll. Set inside a sprawling former courthouse, it has four bars, a huge stage and a welcoming atmosphere. For those with a preference for reggae and hip-hop tunes, events and even live concerts are held during the week (see p70).

5 Nasa

Intimate and exclusive, Nasa is worth visiting for its bright white, space-age decor. They play a good mix of music, from uplifting house to modern soul with a retro twist. Dress elegantly in order to gain entry to this chic club (see p70).

6 Gefährlich

Located in the heart of Norrebro, known for its club culture, Gefährlich (German for "dangerous") has a restaurant, bar, art gallery, coffee shop, boutique and record store. Its nightclub caters to the tastes of the young and hip (see p81).

Nasa

For more nightlife venues, see pp70, 81.

Club Mambo

7 VEGA
Housed in a 1950s trade union building, the club exudes a distinctly Scandinavian atmosphere. It attracts an impressive list of international acts and DJs. The Ideal Bar is on the ground floor. ◈ *Map B6 • Enghavevej 40 • 33 25 70 11 • Nightclub: Open 11pm–5am Fri–Sat • Free till 1am • www.vega.dk*

8 Culture Box
This purist techno club is one of Copenhagen's leading venues for electronic music. ◈ *Map K2 • Kronprinsessegade 54 • 33 32 50 50 • Open 11pm–5am Fri–Sat • www.culture-box.com*

9 Stengade 30
Essentially a rock venue, it also has a jazz club and hosts club nights in its dark, graffiti-daubed ground floor. RubA'Dub Sundays are very popular weekly nights of reggae and dancehall. ◈ *Map C3 • Stengade 18 • 35 36 09 38 • Open 9pm–2am Tue & Wed, 9pm–5am Thu, 10pm–5am Fri–Sun • www. stengade30.dk*

10 Club Mambo
If you want to "feel the Latin spirit", then this is the place to be at. An energetic and colourful club, it is one of the hottest salsa clubs in the city. Take advantage of the hour long, free salsa and merengue classes on offer at the club (see p70).

Top 10 Microbreweries

1 Jacobsens
Dedicated to the development of connoisseur beers. ◈ *Gammel Carlsbergvej 11, Valby • 33 27 12 82 • www.jacobsenbryg.dk*

2 Nørrebro Bryghus
Take a tour of the brewery; taste some beer. ◈ *Ryesgade 3, Nørrebro • 35 30 05 30 • www.noerrebrobryghus.dk*

3 Vesterbro Bryghus
Five beers brewed to traditional Austrian recipes. ◈ *Vesterbrogade 2 • 33 11 17 05 • www.vesterbrobryghus.dk*

4 Færgekroen
Two hand-brewed beers on offer. ◈ *Tivoli • 33 75 06 80 • www.faergekroen.dk*

5 Brewpub
Beer garden in a lovely 17th-century building. ◈ *Vestergade 29 • 33 32 00 60 • Closed Sun • www.brewpub.dk*

6 Bryggeriet Apollo
One of the original local microbreweries. ◈ *Vesterbrogade Tivoli 3 • 33 12 33 13 • www.bryggeriet.dk*

7 Brøckhouse
20,000 litres (42,000 pints) of beer brewed per month. ◈ *Højgevej 6, Hillerød • 48 24 24 60 • www.broeckhouse.dk*

8 GourmetBryggeriet
Seasonally brewed beer. ◈ *Bytoften 10–12, Roskilde • 46 32 60 45 • www. gourmetbryggeriet.dk*

9 Fuglebjerggaard
Organic microbrewery. ◈ *Hemmingstrupvej 8, Helsingor • 48 39 39 43*

10 Amager Bryghus
Two-hour tours of this microbrewery take place Thu–Sat. ◈ *Fuglebaekvej 2c • 32 50 62 00 • www.amagerbryghus.dk*

Left **Centralhjørnet** Right **Masken Bar & Café**

Gay and Lesbian Venues

Centralhjørnet
This is Copenhagen's first gay bar. It holds drag nights; regular shows take place on Thursdays. Kylie Minogue and Europop are jukebox favourites. Sunday afternoons are usually packed. ⑧ Map H4 • Kattesundet 18 • 33 11 85 49 • Open noon–2am • www.centralhjornet.dk

Dunkel
The atmospheric lighting (Dunkel means "slightly dark" in Danish) and stuffed owls on the ceiling are set off by the electronic music that bounces off the black walls. The broad beer selection caters to the hip young crowd. ⑧ Map H5 • Vester Voldgade 10 • 33 14 13 30 • Open 4pm–5am Tue–Sat

Jailhouse
Kitted out as a prison, this café and event bar has booths like prison cells and staff dressed as prison guards or police officers. There is a restaurant on the second floor; the atmosphere here is more sedate.
⑧ Map H4 • Studiestræde 12 • 33 15 22 55 • Open 3pm–2am Sun–Thu, 3pm–5am Fri–Sat; Restaurant: 6–11pm Thu–Sat • www.jailhousecph.dk

Oscar Bar and Café
A bar and café for the style-conscious, it has a 2-m (almost 7-ft) long bar and posh leather furniture. The DJ plays funky disco and soulful deep house on weekends. ⑧ Map H5 • Rådhus pladsen 77 • 33 12 09 99 • Open noon–2am (kitchen till 10pm) • www.oscarbarcafe.dk

Café Intime's Piano Bar
Founded in 1913, this kitsch bar has a predominantly gay crowd. A pianist plays popular classics (don't be afraid to sing along); you can also enjoy jazz on Sundays. ⑧ Map B5 • Allégade 25, 2000 Frederiksberg • 38 34 19 58 • Open 6pm–2am • www.cafeintime.dk

Amigo Bar
This popular downtown bar pulsates with a lively party atmosphere well into the early hours. Its speciality is camp karaoke. ⑧ Map C5 • Schønbergsgade 4, 2000 Frederiksberg • 33 21 49 15 • Open 10pm–7am daily

K3
This three-storey "pansexual" club caters to a range of crowds during the week, with four

Jailhouse

Oscar Bar and Café

rooms, two dance floors and electronic pop from the 1970s, '80s and '90s blasting out of the sound system. There is a minimum age limit of 24 on Saturdays. ✆ *Map J4 • Knabostræde 3 • 33 14 13 30 • Open 10pm–6am • www.k-3.dk*

8 Mens Bar
This strictly all-male, no-frills bar is filled with leather, fascinating tattoos and a dash of denim. Try to catch the free Danish brunch at 3pm on the first Sunday of the month. ✆ *Map H4 • Teglgardsstræde 3 • 33 12 73 03 • Open 3pm–2am • www.mensbar.dk*

9 Masken Bar & Café
The younger crowd at this venue starts buzzing after midnight. It has exciting live music and drag shows, spread across two floors. ✆ *Map H4 • Studiestræde 33 • 33 91 09 37 • Open 4pm–2am Mon–Thu, 4pm–5am Fri, 3pm–5am Sat, 3pm–2am Sun • www.maskenbar.dk*

10 Meet Gay Copenhagen
You can meet and dine with local gays and lesbians in the comfort of their homes. Hosts are very friendly and usually offer traditional fare. It's best to book a dinner well in advance. Note: this is not a dating agency. ✆ *27 21 80 65 • www.meetgaycopenhagen.dk*

Top 10 Gay & Lesbian Festivals & Events

1 Copenhagen Gay & Lesbian Film Festival
10-day film festival, usually in October, at various venues. ✆ *33 93 07 66 • www.cglff.dk*

2 Copenhagen Pride Festival
Week-long festival in August. Includes the gay pride parade. ✆ *www.copenhagenpride.dk*

3 Mr Gay
Pan Club's popular, good-humoured beauty pageant for gays. ✆ *www.mrgay.dk*

4 Rainbow Festival
10 days of art exhibitions, drag shows, dancing and parades just across the bridge at Malmö, Sweden. ✆ *www.rfsl.se/malmo*

5 Gloria Goes Gay
Screens gay and lesbian films every Monday. ✆ *Rådhuspladsen 59 • 33 12 42 92 • www.gloria.dk*

6 Copenhagen Mermates
Swimming club hosting the World Outgames (gay sport and cultural event) in 2009. ✆ *www.mermates.dk/2007*

7 Nordic Open
Dance competition for same-sex couples on 30 December every year. ✆ *www.pandans.dk/nordicopen.htm*

8 World AIDS Day
This event in memory of people who have died of AIDS takes place on the last Sunday in May. ✆ *www.aidsfondet.dk*

9 St. Hans
Annual bonfire and beach party on Amager Beach on 23 June. ✆ *www.lbl.dk*

10 Queer Festival
Musicians, activists and drag kings and queens take part. ✆ *www.queerfestival.org*

Left **Children's Museum at the Nationalmuseet** Right **Classic car rides, Tivoli**

Places for Children

Guinness World Records Museum

1 Guinness World Records Museum

This highly popular attraction brings the Guinness World Records to life. From the bizarre, such as bicycle-eating men to the internationally renowned in sport and science, 13 galleries celebrate strangeness, ingenuity and determination *(see p66)*.

2 Statens Museum for Kunst

The Children's Art Museum of the Danish National Gallery holds exhibitions for children between the ages of 6 and 12. Artist-led workshops are designed to allow children to develop ideas in response to art at the museum *(see pp22–3)*.

3 Wonderful World of HC Andersen Museum

Explore the life of Hans Christian Andersen, Denmark's national hero, at this charming museum. It is aimed at kids who will enjoy the tableaux and recordings of some of his fairytales (in several languages). The handwritten manuscript of *The Stone and the Wise Man* (1858) may interest bibliophiles *(see p66)*.

4 Nationalmuseet

The National Museum includes an interesting Children's Museum. Rather than just looking at things, children are encouraged to participate in numerous activities, like dressing up in grandma's clothes to see how different they are from today's garments, or sitting in an old Danish classroom, learning about medieval castles *(see pp26–7)*.

5 Tøjhusmuseet

The Royal Arsenal Museum, on the island of Slotsholmen, is a popular tourist site and is home to Christian IV's original arsenal (1604–8). The ground floor, in particular, evokes the atmosphere of those days, with a long arched cavern and canons along walls *(see p28)*.

Hands-on fun for kids at Experimentarium

6 Experimentarium

This innovative science centre brings science to life through hands-on exploration. Almost every exhibit is interactive, giving kids the chance to perform 300 different experiments. Environmental issues are high on the agenda and adults will have as much fun as kids (see p97).

7 Danmarks Akvarium

Over 70 tanks of the world's most exotic fish are found here. Touch-tanks let you get closer to the safer marine life. Turtles, piranhas and sharks are the star attractions (see p99).

Dried seahorse, Danish Akvarium

8 Zoologisk Have

This delightful zoo is Denmark's largest cultural institution, attracting around 1.2 million visitors every year. Besides the fauna like the tigers, polar bears, and elephants, there are also thematic adventure trails and a children's zoo where animals can be petted. In spring, there tend to be many new baby animals to excite the children (see p83).

9 Tivoli

The best time to take kids to Tivoli is during the day, when the atmosphere is more family-oriented and there are fewer adults around. There are plenty of fun rides, including cars on tracks, dragon boats on the lake, the pantomime theatre and the trolley bus. There are plenty of changing facilities, and you won't have a hard time finding child-friendly places to eat either (see pp10–13).

10 Ripley's Believe It or Not!

While adults may find the collection of bizarre, freakish curiosities on display here a little unsettling, kids are sure to love it! The Ecuadorian shrunken heads are a particularly gruesome highlight. ⊗ Map H5
• Rådhuspladsen 57 • 33 32 31 31
• Open 10am–6pm daily (to 8pm Fri–Sat)
• Adm; Copenhagen Card accepted

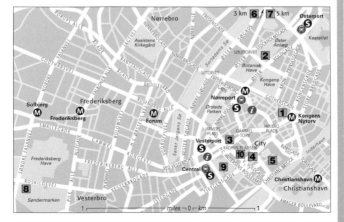

Left **Christian VIII's Palace, Amalienborg** Right **Vor Frue Kirke, detail of façade**

TOP 10 Sights of Royal Copenhagen

1 Amalienborg

This royal residence consists of four palaces arranged around a square. The sovereign's home is closed to the public. You can visit other sections during the tourist season. Queen Margrethe resides in Christian IX's Palace and Crown Prince Frederik in Frederik VIII's Palace. An interesting museum housed in Christian VIII's Palace includes reconstructed rooms from the 19th century. *(see pp20–21).*

2 Rosenborg Slot

This delightful, turreted Renaissance palace, built by Christian IV, is the oldest royal palace standing in its original form. It is also a depository for the crown jewels *(see pp14–15).*

3 Royal Copenhagen Porcelain

This was one of the first porcelain factories outside Germany.

Christiansborg Slot

The traditional Royal Copenhagen design, "Blue Floral", dates back to the factory's initiation in 1775. The pottery features a blue design because in earlier times, cobalt was the only colour that was able to withstand high firing temperatures *(see p64).*

4 Vor Frue Kirke

St. Mary's Cathedral has been a place of royal worship and ceremony since the 12th century, when Margrethe I married Håkon IV of Norway. Since then, Christian I (1449) and Crown Prince Frederik (2004) have been married here and several princes have been crowned *(see p17).*

5 Christiansborg Slot

This is the seventh castle to have been built upon this site. The first, Bishop Absalon's fortified castle (1167), was destroyed in 1369. It has since been rebuilt several times. The castle built in 1730 was the first to be called Christiansborg; it was destroyed by fire 64 years later *(see p28).*

6 Crown Jewels

These symbols of monarchy, kept in the stronghold basement of Rosenborg Slot, include the crown, sceptre, orb, sword of state, ampulla (flask for anointing the monarch) and royal jewellery.

7 Fredensborg Slot

This 18th-century Baroque palace is the Queen's summer

Rosenborg Slot

and autumn home. The beautiful gardens are among Denmark's largest. 🕾 *33 40 31 87 • Open only in Jul 1pm–4:30pm; Reserved gardens, 9am–5pm • Adm; Free entry to gardens • Bus 173E, direction Fredensborg*

8 Frederiksborg Slot
Christian IV built this Dutch Renaissance-style castle between 1600–20. It is notable for its spires, copper roofs and sweeping gables. After being destroyed in a fire in 1859, the Carlsberg Brewery magnate, Jacob Jacobsen, helped rebuild it. The gardens, dating to 1720–25, were the only royal gardens to have escaped being updated to the 19th-century Romantic style *(see p99)*.

9 Roskilde Domkirke
Danish royals, including Harald Bluetooth *(see p33)*, have been buried here since the 12th century. It now houses 39 tombs, the oldest belonging to Margrethe I (d. 1412) *(see p100)*.

10 Kronborg Slot
This castle, built as a fortress in the 15th century, was used as a prison and army barracks until 1922. It is now occasionally used for royal functions. You may even hear a salute being fired whenever the royal yacht passes by *(see p102)*.

The Treasury

1 Christian IV's Crown
Made in 1595–96 by Dirich Fyring, with diamond, gold, enamel and pearls.

2 The Queen's Crown
Made for Queen Sophie Magdalene in 1731. The large, square table-cut diamonds are believed to have come from Queen Sophie Amalie's crown (1648).

3 Christian V's Crown
Christian V's Absolutist crown (1670–71). Its large, rare sapphire is believed to be a present from the Duke of Milan to Christian I in 1474.

4 The Regalia
Sceptre, orb, globe and ampulla made for Frederik III's coronation. Used at subsequent coronations until 1840.

5 Order of the Elephant
Founded by Christian I around 1450. The chain is made of gold, enamel, diamonds and pearls.

6 Order of the Dannebrog
Established in 1671 as part of the measures introduced by the Absolute monarchs to manage their subjects.

7 Jewellery Sets
Includes pearl set (1840), made from Charlotte Amalie's jewellery; diamond set (18th century); emerald set (1723).

8 The Oldenburg Horn
Enamelled, silver-gilt drinking horn (around 1465).

9 The King's Law 1665
Absolutism's constitution, made from parchment, silk, gold and silver.

10 Baptismal Set
Four-piece, gold and silver baptismal set (1671), thought to have been first used for Crown Prince Frederik.

AROUND TOWN

COPENHAGEN'S TOP 10

Left **Ny Carlsberg Glyptotek** Right **Kongens Nytorv**

Tivoli North to Gothersgade

RICH IN HISTORY, *this area is a popular entertainment destination. Heading north-northeast of Tivoli, which was originally outside the city walls, you can walk back in time through the old town that evolved during the Middle Ages – though much of it succumbed to fire in the 18th century – to Slotsholmen, the site where the first dwellings that became Copenhagen were built in the 12th century. Along the way, you will find great shopping areas, museums, an old town and a royal palace.*

🔟 Sights

1. Tivoli
2. Rådhuset
3. Astronomical Clock
4. Ny Carlsberg Glyptotek
5. Nationalmuseet
6. Dansk Design Centre
7. Royal Copenhagen Porcelain Museum
8. Latin Quarter
9. Kongens Nytorv and Nyhavn
10. Slotsholmen

Dansk Design Centre

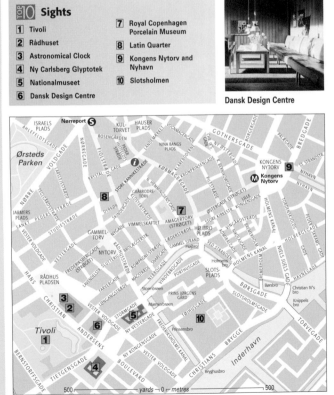

Preceding pages: **Marmorkirken and Amalienborg, seen from Amaliehaven.**

The Tivoli Palace

Astronomical Clock

3 This ingenious clock, cased in a mahogany cabinet, was designed in 1872 by locksmith and watchmaker Jens Olsen. After waiting for 50 years to obtain funds, Olsen started working on the clock in 1943. He died two years later, but work continued and the clock was set in motion in 1955. Famous for its accuracy, this 14,000-part watch loses less than a second a century. It shows local time, solar time, sunrise and sunset times, sidereal time, celestial pole movement and the movement of the planets. ◈ *Map H5 • Rådhus, Rådhuspladsen 1 • 33 66 25 82 • Open 8:30am–4:30pm Mon–Fri, 10am–1pm Sat • Adm*

Ny Carlsberg Glyptotek

4 This superb art gallery is home to a fascinating collection of Mediterranean, Classical and Egyptian art and artifacts. Danish and 19th-century French works of art are also on display, including French Impressionist paintings. The museum is housed in a 19th-century building with a splendid cupola, beneath which lies an indoor winter garden, sculptures and water features. The modern wing is a wonderful, light-filled area *(see pp24–5).*

Tivoli

1 Tivoli has virtually become synonymous with Copenhagen and should be high on the list for any visitor. Day or night, this park buzzes with the sounds of exhilarating rides. It is not only for adventure-seekers though. At night, the setting turns magical and romantic, with fairy lights and Japanese lanterns glowing in the darkness and music in the air *(see pp10–11).*

Rådhuset

2 The Copenhagen Rådhus, or town hall, is a mock-Gothic building replete with fantastical sea creatures, built 1892–1905 and designed by architect Martin Nyrop. Its 106.5-m (346-ft) tower affords superb views of the city. Even if you don't want to do the full tour, you could pop in to see the pre-Raphaelitesque entrance way, or the Italianate reception hall. Many Copenhageners get married here, so you may just see several wedding parties on the steps. ◈ *Map H5 • Rådhuspladsen 1 • 33 66 25 82 • Open 7:45am–5pm Mon–Fri, 9:30am–1pm Sat • Tours in English 3pm Mon–Fri, 10am & 11am Sat • www.copenhagencity.dk*

Rådhus

Nationalmuseet
The National Museum is housed inside a former royal residence, dating from the 18th century. The exhibits trace Danish history, from ancient times to the present, including some amazing ethnographic collections. The displays of the popular prehistoric collection on the ground floor are closed until 2008 *(see pp26–7)*.

Dansk Design Center
The Dansk Design Center (DDC) is one of the city's most innovative exhibition organizers. It arranges shows with themes as diverse as Danish Design in Everyday Life to a DJ exhibition that allows visitors to create their own mix on turntables. Housed in a building designed by architect Henning Larsen, its intention is to showcase the use of design in business, while exhibiting Danish innovation. *Map H5 • HC Andersen Boulevard 27–29 • 33 69 33 69 • Open 10am–5pm Mon–Fri (to 9pm Wed), 11am–4pm Sat–Sun • Adm; free 5pm–9pm Wed; free daily for under-12s; free with Copenhagen Card • www.ddc.dk*

Vor Frue Kirke in the Latin Quarter

Royal Copenhagen Porcelain Museet
From November 2007, this museum will have a convenient and central location, as it is being shifted from Vesterbro to the Royal Copenhagen Porcelain shop on Strøget *(see p66)*. Besides presenting historical displays, the museum focuses on the porcelain experience – showing you everything from how to handle porcelain to how to paint your own 'Blue Floral' design *(see p58)*. *Map J4 • Amagertorv 6 • 38 14 96 97 • Open 10am–6pm Mon–Sat (to 7pm Fri, to 5pm Sat), noon–5pm first Sun of month • www.royalcopenhagen.com*

Latin Quarter
To the west of Strøget lies the Latin Quarter, the original home of the Copenhagen University. It dates back to the Middle Ages when the primary language of culture and education was Latin. Some of the old university buildings are still in use, although much of the campus is now on the island of Amager. If you take a left off Strøget onto Nørregade, you will find the Universitetet and Vor Frue Kirke. Both have been used for their current purposes since the 15th and 13th centuries respectively; the current buildings, however, date back to the 19th century. The Rundetårn on Købmagergade is also worth a visit *(see pp16–17)*.

Kongens Nytorv and Nyhavn
At the top of Nyhavn stands the King's New Square (Kongens Nytorv), an elegant area surrounded by fashionable 18th-century mansions that now house banks, upmarket department stores and hotels. It is flanked

Teatermuseet in Slotsholmen

Slot (now an exhibition space) and the Royal Theatre (Det Kongelige Teater) *(see p18)*. Nyhavn (which means "new harbour") is a lively tourist area filled with restaurants, cafés and old sailing boats along the canal quayside. The atmosphere here is a stark contrast to what it was in the 1670s, when sailors, traders and low-lifes frequented the area. Even until 40 years ago, this was not a part of town that many would have visited at night. Urban regeneration has changed all that and on sunny evenings in particular, you may not find a place to sit down *(see pp18–19)*.

10 Slotsholmen

A visit to Slotsholmen could take up almost an entire day, as there is plenty to see. Primarily the site of Christiansborg Slot (you can visit the state rooms on a guided tour) which burnt down in 1794, it is now home to Denmark's Parliament. You will find several museums here as well for the tourist looking for a bit of culture. The delightful Theatre Museum (Teatermuseet) *(see p35)* is definitely worth a visit with the main attraction being the 18th-century palace theatre. Other sites include the palace church and the 12th-century ruins of the first Copenhagen castle where its founder, Bishop Absalon, resided *(see pp28–9)*.

Walking Tour

Morning

Start your day at the **Ny Carlsberg Glyptotek** *(see p63)*; don't miss the impressive Egyptian and Impressionist collections. Have an early lunch at the charming **Winter Garden Café** *(see pp24–5)*.

Afternoon

After lunch, cross HC Andersen Boulevard and visit the **Dansk Design Center** or head to the **Nationalmuseet** and take one of the hour-long tours. Then, stroll to the end of Ny Vestergade until you reach Frederiks Kanal. Cross the bridge and visit **Christiansborg Slot** *(see p28)*. If you arrive by 2pm, pop into the stables, the **Teatermuseet** *(see p35)* and the ruins before taking a tour of the state rooms at 3pm. Then, walk back over the bridge and turn right to Gammel Strand (note the **Fishwife statue**, *see p37)* for afternoon snacks at one of the restaurants and cafés. Walk down Købmagergade via Højbro Plads, right up to **Rundetårn** *(see p16)*. If you are feeling energetic, hike to the top for a good view of the city. Heading back down, take a left from Strøget and keep walking until you reach **Kongens Nytorv and Nyhavn** – a perfect spot for a relaxing evening drink and supper at one of the quayside bars and restaurants. Instead of heading back via Strøget, take the less mainstream Lille Strandstræde. Walk to Rådhuspladsen and go across to **Tivoli** *(see p63)*. Spend the evening at these lovely gardens enjoying the atmosphere.

Left **Erotica Museum** Centre **Caritasspringvandet** Right **The Royal Copenhagen shop on Strøget**

TOP 10 Best of the Rest

1 Domhuset
The city's local courthouse was built between 1805–15. The "Bridge of Sighs" across Slutterigade (prison street) gets its name from the prisoners being led across it for trial. ◈ *Map H4 • Nytorv 25 • Open 8:30am–4:30pm Mon–Thu, 8:30am–3pm Fri*

2 Rådhuspladsen
On the edge of Tivoli, the town hall square is one of the liveliest areas of the city. ◈ *Map H5*

3 Statue of HC Andersen
This statue of the author by Henry Lukow-Nielsen was unveiled in 1961. ◈ *Map H5*

4 Caritasspringvandet
Dating back to 1608, the Charity Fountain is one of the oldest in the city. ◈ *Map H4*

5 Guinness World Records Museum
This museum demonstrates 500 Guinness records. ◈ *Map K4 • Østergade 16 • 33 32 31 31 • Open Sep–mid-Jun 10am–6pm daily (to 8pm Fri–Sat); mid-Jun–Aug 10am–10pm daily • Adm; free with Copenhagen Card • www.guinness.dk*

6 Wonderful World of HC Andersen Museum
Scenes from Andersen's fairy tales and other memorabilia are found here. ◈ *Map H5 • Rådhuspladsen 57 • 33 32 31 31 • Open Sep–mid-Jun 10am–6pm Sun–Thu, 10am–8pm Fri–Sat; mid-Jun–Aug 10am–10pm daily • Adm for adults; free with Copenhagen Card*

7 Post & Telemuseet
Housed inside the main post office, this museum charts the history of modern communication from the 17th century onwards. ◈ *Map J4 • Købmagergade 37 • 33 41 09 00 • Open 10am–5pm Tue–Sat (to 8pm Wed), noon–4pm Sun • Adm; free with Copenhagen Card • www.ptt-museum.dk*

8 Erotica Museum
Includes varied displays from the lives of 19th-century prostitutes to the modern sex industry. ◈ *Map J4 • Købmagergade 24 • Open May–Sept 10am–11pm daily; Oct–Apr 10am–8pm Sun–Thu, 10am–10pm Fri–Sat • Adm; Copenhagen Card accepted • www.museumerotica.dk*

9 Georg Jensen Museum
The jewellery and homeware of the famous silversmith are on display here. ◈ *Map J4 • Amagertorv 4 • 33 14 02 29 • Open 10am–5:30pm Mon–Fri • www.royalcopenhagen.com*

10 Strøget
This is the name given to the five main, interconnected shopping streets of Copenhagen. ◈ *Map H5–K4*

Around Town – Tivoli North to Gothersgade

Price Categories

For a three-course meal for one with half a bottle of wine (or equivalent meal), taxes and extra charges.

⊛	up to Dkr150
⊛⊛	150–200
⊛⊛⊛	200–300
⊛⊛⊛⊛	300–350
⊛⊛⊛⊛⊛	over Dkr350

Riz Raz

🔟 Dining

1 Riz Raz
Riz Raz is famous for its great value, Mediterranean-influenced vegetarian buffets and helpful service. ✆ *Map J5* • *Kom-pagnistræde 20* • *33 15 05 75* • *www.rizraz.dk* • ⊛

2 L'Alsace
This gourmet restaurant specializes in dishes from Alsace, with an emphasis on fresh fish and seafood. ✆ *Map K4* • *Ny Østergade 9* • *33 14 57 43* • *Closed Sun* • *www.alsace.dk* • ⊛⊛⊛

3 Alberto K
One of the best restaurants in Denmark, it offers a blend of Scandinavian-Italian flavours. ✆ *Map G5* • *SAS Radisson Royal Hotel, Hammerichsgade 1* • *33 42 61 61* • *Closed Sun* • *Book ahead* • *www. alberto-k.dk* • ⊛⊛⊛⊛⊛

4 Café à Porta
Once the local eaterie for HC Andersen, this stylish bistro-café is a great place for a cocktail. The food is varied, and the homemade puddings are excellent. ✆ *Map K4* • *Kongens Nytorv 17* • *33 11 05 00* • *Closed Sun* • *www.cafeaporta.dk* • ⊛⊛⊛⊛⊛

5 Ego
Food and drinks in this smart, airy brasserie are beautifully presented. Fish and foie gras preparations are especially good. ✆ *Map K4* • *Hovedvagtsgade 2, off Kongens Nytorv* • *33 12 79 71* • *Closed Sun* • *www.egocph.dk* • ⊛⊛

6 Thorvaldsens Hus
This attractive bistro-style restaurant serves tasty food at decent prices. ✆ *Map J4* • *Gammel Strand 34* • *33 32 04 00* • *www.thorvaldsens-hus.dk* • ⊛⊛⊛

7 Atlas Bar
The exotic dishes on offer here are as interesting as the cool basement location. ✆ *Map H4* • *Larsbjørnsstræde 18* • *33 15 03 52* • ⊛

8 Bankeråt
Enjoy steaks, salads and a selection of beers in this artistic venue. ✆ *Map G3* • *Ahlefeldtsgade 29* • *33 93 69 88* • *www.bankeraat.dk* • ⊛

9 Ida Davidsen
Choose from 250 top-quality, handmade open sandwiches. ✆ *Map K3* • *Store Kongensgade 70* • *33 91 36 55* • *Closed Sun & public holidays* • *www.idadavidsen.dk* • ⊛⊛⊛

10 Husmanns Vinstue
This wine cellar/pub/restaurant offers many traditional herring-based dishes. ✆ *Map H4* • *Larsbjørnsstræde 2* • *33 11 58 86* • *Closed Sun* • *www.husmannsvinstue.dk* • ⊛⊛

Left **Birger Christensen** Centre **Illum Department Store** Right **Royal Copenhagen shop**

Strøget Shopping

1 Illums Bolighus
This shrine to stylish interior design and kitchenware (mainly Italian and Danish) offers everything from Royal Copenhagen porcelain and art objects to groovy dog-biscuit dispensers. A wonderful selection of objects of art can make great wedding presents. ◊ *Map J4* • *Amagertorv 10* • *33 14 19 41* • *www.royalshopping.com*

2 Royal Copenhagen
This flagship store offers a range of designs, from the classic 18th-century *flora danica* design to the modern and organic. ◊ *Map J4* • *Amagertorv 6* • *33 13 71 81* • *Closed Sun* • *www.royalcopenhagen.com*

3 Illum Department Store
This stylish, six-storied de-partment store offers quality clothing and homeware. There is also a café, bakery and a supermarket. ◊ *Map K4* • *Østergade 52* • *33 14 40 02* • *Closed Sun* • *www.illum.dk*

4 Birger Christensen
This exclusive fashion store sells Birger Christensen fur coats and jackets, as well as a wide collection of international labels. ◊ *Map K4* • *Østergade 38* • *33 11 55 55* • *Closed Sun, second & third Sat* • *www.birger-christensen.com*

5 Georg Jensen
Georg Jensen's superb designs are available here, including stylish jewellery, watches, cutlery, candlesticks, antiques and even designer sunglasses. If you are interested in the Jensen antiques, you can have your pick from the basement. ◊ *Map J4* • *Amagertorv 4* • *33 11 40 80* • *Closed Sat & Sun* • *www.georgjensen.com*

6 Bodum
Famous for its coffee cups and glass cafetières, Bodum sells a range of stylish, modern kitchenware. The second floor houses a trendy range of cards. ◊ *Map K4* • *Østergade 10* • *33 36 40 80* • *www.bodum.com*

7 Noa Noa
Offers women's cottons, linens and silks in pretty styles and a similar collection for girls aged 3–12. ◊ *Map K4* • *Østergade 16* • *33 13 06 08* • *www.noa-noa.dk*

8 Rosenthal
This avant-garde gallery has a range of gift and art objects. ◊ *Map H5* • *Frederiksberggade 21* • *33 14 21 01* • *www.rosenthal.dk*

9 A Pair
Here you will find fashionable footwear for men and women. Leather bags and belts with large, silver buckles are also available. ◊ *Map K4* • *Ny Østergade 3* • *33 91 99 20* • *www.apair.dk*

10 Sand
This Danish fashion house offers a range of stylish and classic clothing and accessories for both men and women. ◊ *Map K4* • *Østergade 40* • *33 14 21 21* • *www.sand-europe.com*

Strøget has no street sign: it's local for Frederiksberggade, Nygade, Vimmelskaftet, Amagertorv and Østergade combined.

Left **Sneaky Fox boutique** Right **Magasin du Nord**

Shops Off Strøget

Munthe Plus Simonsen
1 This award-winning Danish design duo offers wearable women's clothing and accessories with a stylish edge. ❧ *Map K4 • Grennegade 10 • 33 32 03 12 • www.muntheplussimonsen.com*

Boutique Isabel
2 At this saucy sex shop, you will find a wide selection of lingerie, toys and costumes. ❧ *Map H4 • Sankt Pederstræde 35 • 33 13 43 13 • www.boutique-isabel.dk*

Magasin du Nord
3 This is one of the city's oldest department stores, offering an upmarket selection of clothing and homeware. Also here are a supermarket and plenty of places to eat. The discount sales held in January and late summer are very good. ❧ *Map K4 • Kongens Nytorv 13 • 33 11 44 33 • Closed Sun (except first Sun of the month) • www.magasin.dk*

Sneaky Fox
4 This trendy women's boutique is especially well-known for its vast variety of different types of stockings, from the silly to the sophisticated. ❧ *Map H4 • Larsbjørnsstræde 15 • 33 91 25 20 • www.sneakyfox.dk*

Jane Buchard
5 You will find fabulous designer cloth handbags here, unique in their Baroque excesses and craftsmanship. ❧ *Map J4 • Købmagergade 7 • 33 15 33 88 • www.janeburchard.com*

Grønlykke
6 Visit this funky shop if you are looking for colourful and kitsch household accessories, from kitchen bar stools to chandeliers. You will also find an assorted range of knick-knacks and bags. ❧ *Map J4 • Læderstræde 3 • 33 13 00 81 • www.gronlykke.com*

Crème de la Crème à la Edgar
7 Lovely (though expensive) children's wear, toys and accessories are available here. ❧ *Map J4 • Kompagnistræde 8 • 33 36 18 18 • www.cremedelacremealaedgar.dk*

Akimbo
8 This is a great place for pre-sents, especially for little girls, ranging from edible-looking candle cakes, to jewellery and kitsch toys. ❧ *Map J4 • Hyskenstræde 3 • 33 11 13 01*

Wettergren and Wettergren
9 Hidden away down a few steps leading to a basement, this charming shop sells vintage clothing and accessories with a modern twist. ❧ *Map J4 • Læderstræde 5 • 33 13 14 05*

Stilleben
10 This tiny shop is filled with beautiful porcelain ceramics, available in a range of subtle colours, all created by young Danish potters and ceramic designers. ❧ *Map J4 • Læderstræde 14 • 33 91 11 31 • www.stilleben.dk*

Left **Café Ketchup** Right **Intoxica Tiki Bar & Kitchen**

 # TOP 10 Nightlife

1 Studenterhuset
This charmingly grotty bar serves beer to students at discounted prices, while local bands dish out some good music. ◎ Map J3 • Købmagergade 52 • 35 32 38 61 • www.studenterhuset.com

2 The Rock
Set in an old courthouse, this rock venue hosts great live rock shows. There are four bars and the nightclub is open until dawn. ◎ Map H4 • Skindergade 45–47 • 33 91 39 13 • www.the-rock.dk

3 Nasa
This exclusive club has a posh interior, top-notch DJs and great dance music. ◎ Map K3 • Gothersgade 8F • 33 93 74 15 • Open midnight–6am Fri–Sat • www.nasa.dk

4 Grand Teatret
This large, six-screen art house cinema has a smart, comfortable atmosphere. The Grand Café hosts cultural evenings. ◎ Map H5 • Mikkel Bryggersgade 8 • 33 15 16 11 • www.grandteatret.dk

5 Café Ketchup
Stylish and slick, this café-restaurant offers fabulous food (a combination of Danish and oriental) and cocktails. ◎ Map J3 • Pilestraede 19 • 33 32 30 30 • Closed Sun • www.cafeketchup.dk

6 Bar Rouge
This is one of the hippest cocktail bars in the city, with tastefully designed interiors. The menu offers an extensive list of cocktails. ◎ Map H4 • In Hotel Skt Petri, Krystalgade 22 • 33 45 98 22 • www.hotelsktpetri.com/barrouge

7 Luux
Set in a former jazz club, this is a classy, deep-house-loving club. ◎ Map H4 • Nørregade 41 • 33 13 67 88 • 11pm–5am Thu–Fri, 11pm–5am Sat • www.luux.dk

8 Copenhagen Jazz House
This live jazz venue attracts both international bands and home-grown talent. ◎ Map J4 • Niels Hemmingsensgade 10 • 33 15 26 00 • www.jazzhouse.dk

9 Intoxica Tiki Bar & Kitchen
At night, this restaurant turns into a lively cocktail bar with some of Copenhagen's top bartenders. ◎ Map G4 • Jarmers Plads 3 • 33 38 70 30 • www.intoxica.dk

10 Club Mambo
Dance to salsa in the club, or visit the lounge for some reggae and modern hits. ◎ Map H5 • Vester Voldgade 85 • 33 11 97 66 • www.clubmambo.dk

Price Categories

For a three-course meal for one with half a bottle of wine (or equivalent meal), taxes and extra charges.

Ⓚ	up to Dkr150
ⓀⓀ	150–200
ⓀⓀⓀ	200–300
ⓀⓀⓀⓀ	300–350
ⓀⓀⓀⓀⓀ	over Dkr350

Charlie's Bar

🔟 Historic Wining and Dining

1 Vandkunsten Sandwich Bar

This popular sandwich bar is housed in what was formerly Copenhagen's oldest butcher's shop. 🅢 Map J5 • Rådhusstræde 17 • 33 13 90 40 • www.vandkunsten sandwich.dk • Ⓚ

2 Skindbuksen

Founded in 1728, mariners, locals and tourists now rub shoulders at this unpretentious restaurant. 🅢 Map K4 • Lille Kongensgade 4 • 33 12 90 37 • Book ahead • www.skindbuksen.dk • ⓀⓀⓀ

3 Oonaco

A traditional café, Oonaco is housed in the Stelling Building, designed by Arne Jacobsen in 1937. 🅢 Map H4 • Gammeltorv 6 • 32 13 06 06 • ⓀⓀ

4 Dan Turéll

One of the city's oldest cafés, it has a Parisian-style decor. 🅢 Map K3 • Store Regnegade 3–5 • 33 14 10 47 • www.danturell.dk • ⓀⓀⓀ

5 The Royal Café

This café has outdoor seating and a special menu with "smushi". This fun food combines traditional Danish smørrebrød in bitesize portions, with sushi. 🅢 Map J4 • Amagertorv 6 • 38 14 95 27 • ⓀⓀⓀ

6 Husmanns Vinstue

Once a stable, this comfortable, wood-panelled lunch venue serves tasty traditional Danish fare (see p67).

7 Hviids Vinstue

Copenhagen's oldest wine bar (established 1723), it was one of HC Andersen's favourites. 🅢 Map K4 • Kongens Nytorv 19 • 33 15 10 64 • www.hviidsvinstue.dk • ⓀⓀ

8 Charlie's Bar

Copenhagen's only Cask Marque pub, it serves eighteen independent beers on tap. Danish breads are Hancock and Porse Guld. 🅢 Map J4 • Pilestræde 33 • 33 22 22 89 • www.charlies.dk

9 Perch's Tea Room

Not much seems to have changed since 1834, when AC Perch started importing fine teas. Weighed on scales, the tea is brewed with reverence. 🅢 Map J4 • Kronprinsensgade 5 • 33 15 35 77 • Closed Sun • www.perchs.dk

10 Restaurant Parnas

Opened in the 1930s, it has retained a comfortable, rustic, traditional feel. The cuisine is typically Danish; try their speciality, Parnas Gryde. 🅢 Map K4 • Lille Kongensgade 16 • 60 19 57 05 • Book ahead • www.parnas.aok.dk • ⓀⓀ

Left **Rosenborg Slot** Right **Marmorkirken**

Nørrebro, Østerbro and North of Gothersgade

OF THESE THREE NEIGHBOURHOODS, *two are recent additions to the original Copenhagen site, which took up what is now called the "Inner City". Nørrebro, northeast of the Inner City, lies across the Dronning Louises Bro (Queen Louise's Bridge). Until the 19th century, this area was mainly farmland; today it is a lively, multicultural part of the city with plenty of bars, cafés and alternative shopping centres. Østerbro, slightly northeast of Nørrebro, has remained an uncluttered, suburban residential area since the 19th century. The train station, Østerport, was built in 1894–97 to help workers travel to the city centre, on the site of Copenhagen's fortified eastern gate. The area north of Gothersgade is part of the Inner City and takes in later parts of the original capital dating back to the Renaissance period.*

Frihedsmuseet

🔟 Sights

1. Assistens Kirkegård
2. Botanisk Have
3. Statens Museum for Kunst
4. Den Hirschprungske Samling
5. Rosenborg Slot and Kongens Have
6. Davids Samling
7. Amalienborg
8. Marmorkirken
9. Kunstindustrimuseet
10. Frihedsmuseet

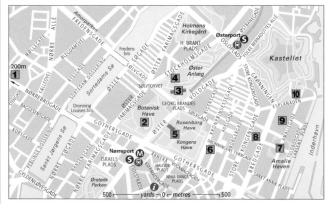

Preceding pages: **Christmas at Tivoli, the Chinese Pagoda.**

1 Assistens Kirkegård

If you are not a devoted fan of dead famous Danes, this cemetery may not be top of your list. However, it is a wonderful place to relax or take a romantic walk. The churchyard is beautiful and is located in the trendy Nørrebro district. ✎ Map C3
• Kapelvej 2 • 35 37 19 17 • Open May–Aug 8am–8pm daily; Sep–Oct, Mar–Apr, 8am–6pm daily; Nov–Feb 8am–4pm daily
• www.assistens.dk

2 Botanisk Have

Among the prettiest outdoor spaces in the city, these gardens are studded with lakes, bridges and lovely flowerbeds. Climb the winding staircase for a great view of the exotic trees below. A geological and botanical museum are also here. ✎ Map H2–J2
• Gothersgade 130 • 35 32 22 21 • Open May–Sep 8:30am–6pm daily; Oct–Apr 8:30am–4pm Tue–Sun, closed Mon, 24 Dec & 1 Jan • www.botanic-garden.ku.dk

3 Statens Museum for Kunst

The National Gallery has an impressive collection of both national and international art, including works by the Old Masters and popular modern icons such as Matisse and Picasso (see pp22–3).

Statens Museum for Kunst

4 Den Hirschsprungske Samling

This small art gallery is situated just behind the National Gallery and displays the collection of tobacco magnate, Heinrich Hirschsprung, given to the nation in 1902. Housed in a 19th-century building, the collection is fittingly dedicated to 19th- and early 20th-century Danish art, including works by painters of the "Golden Age" and the Impressionistic Skagen School, whose signature style involved the use of bright colours and patchy brushwork. Contemporary furniture is also showcased at this museum.
✎ Map J1 • Stockholmsgade 20 • 35 42 03 06 • Open 11am–4pm Wed–Mon
• Adm for adults; free Wed, free with Copenhagen Card • www.hirschsprung.dk

Botanisk Have

5 Rosenborg Slot and Kongens Have

Rosenborg Castle and King's Garden are among the city's highlights, especially on sunny days when the park is full of people and entertainment. Rosenborg Slot was built in 1606–34 on what was then the outskirts of the city. Today it is the only castle in the city centre that has not succumbed to fire. As a result, little has changed about the structure since the time the royal family inhabited it in the 17th and 18th centuries (see pp14–15).

6 Davids Samling

This museum holds the lovely private art collection that belonged to supreme court barrister and art lover, CL David. The collection includes European decorative arts from the 18th and 19th centuries, as well as a fine range of Islamic art and artifacts. Set in an elegant, 19th-century town house, it is interes-ting to see the art collection in a contemporaneous setting. The museum is currently under restoration and will re-open in May 2008. ⊗ Map K3
• Kronprinsessegade 30–32 • 33 73 49 49
• Open 10am–4pm daily (closed until May 2009) • www.davidmus.dk

7 Amalienborg

If you wish to look around inside the royal palaces, you need to visit on a weekend in summer. If you are unable to do so, you can only visit certain parts of the palace that have been set up as a museum. Either way, the Amalienborg complex is worth looking at from the outside. The palaces were built as an important part of an 18th-century aristocratic district and are very different from the narrow streets and houses of the old quarter. When it was first built, it was visually linked to the Marble Church (see below); the modern Opera House (see p8) and the new construction across the harbour on Holmen offer a contemporary visual contrast (see pp20–21).

8 Marmorkirken

Standing close to the Amalienborg is the splendid Marmorkirken (Marble Church), a part of the great architectural design for the Frederiksstad area. However, plans for its construction were so extravagant that finances ran out and work was abandoned in 1770. For more than a century, it stood as a picturesque ruin before being rescued and financed by

Amalienborg

Kunstindustrimuseet

a Danish industrialist. It was in 1894 that the church was finally completed *(see pp20–21)*.

9 Kunstindustrimuseet

The National Museum of Decorative Art and Design is a great place to visit if you are interested in either modern Danish design (everything from colanders and motorbikes to cardboard chairs) or the decorative arts of Europe, China and Japan. The museum also includes a poster and print collection, and a fascinating textiles and dress collection.

◉ *Map L2 • Bredgade 68 • 33 18 56 56 • Open 11am–4pm Tue–Sun • Adm for adults; free with Copenhagen Card • www.kunstindustrimuseet.dk*

10 Frihedsmuseet

The Danish Resistance Museum pays tribute to, and tells the stories of, the people who lived in Denmark during the German occupation (1940–45). It explores their daily lives and the resistance activities that they upheld – from underground newspapers and radio stations to sabotage and the rescue of virtually every Jew in Denmark from under the noses of the Germans. ◉ *Map L2 • Churchill-parken 7 • 33 47 39 21 • Open May–Sep 10am–5pm Tue–Sun; Oct–Apr 10am–3pm Tue–Sun • www.natmus.dk*

Walking Tour

Morning

Start your day at the **Den Hirschsprungske Samling** *(see p75)* museum, amongst the Skagen School's Danish Impressionist paintings. Then cross the gardens to the impressive **Statens Museum for Kunst** *(see 75)*; take an audio guide to learn about the displays.

Afternoon

For lunch, stop over at either the museum café or the **Botanisk Have** *(see p75)* café, depending upon the weather. The gardens are a great place for a picnic, too. Don't forget to visit the palm house. Heading out from the gate on Øster Voldgade, cross over to **Rosenborg Slot.** You can spend a few enjoyable hours here, visiting the castle, the crown jewels and strolling through the gardens. Then, leave from the Kronprinsessegade gate and pop into the **Davids Samling** museum for some Islamic art. Walk down Dronningens Tværgade, take a left onto Bredgade and walk right up to **Marmorkirken**. If you are here by 3pm, take a tour up to the tower. Right in front of the church is the **Amalienborg**. Take a walk through it to the pretty banks of the harbour and see the **Opera House** *(see p8)* across the water. If you are up for a 20-minute walk, head toward the **Little Mermaid** *(see p78)*, passing the distinctive **Gefionspringvandet** *(see p78)* and **Frihedsmuseet** (worth a visit). To get back to town, hop on to the No 26 bus from Folke Bernadottes Allé.

Left **Gefionspringvandet** Right **Kastellet**

🔟 Best of the Rest

1 Gefionspringvandet
A dramatic sight, this bronze statue represents the tale of goddess Gefion ploughing enough land to create the island of Zealand *(see p37)*. ✎ *Map M2*

2 Medicinsk Museion
This museum has a vast collection of exhibits (some gruesome) dating back to the 18th century. ✎ *Map L2 • Bredgade 62 • 35 32 38 00 • Tours only 1:30pm, 2:30pm and 3:30pm Wed–Fri, 1pm Sun • Adm for adults • www.mhm.ku.dk*

3 The Little Mermaid (Den Lille Havfrue)
This statue of the heroine of Andersen's fairy tale, *Little Mermaid*, perched on a rock in Copenhagen harbour, has been staring out to sea since 1913. ✎ *Map M1 • Langelinie*

4 Amaliehaven
Filled with box hedges and fountains, this park lies to the east of the Amalienborg, facing the harbour across from the Opera House *(see p20).*

5 Kastellet
This pentagram-shaped fortress was built as protection against the Swedes, but only ever used against the English in 1807. ✎ *Map L1 • 33 47 95 00 • Only grounds open to visitors*

6 Kastelskirken
This military church at Kastellet has been holding services since the 17th century. ✎ *Map L1 • Kastellet • 33 15 65 58 • Open 9am–1pm Mon–Thu, 10am–12pm Fri*

7 St Albans Kirke
Named after St Alban, England's first martyr, this Anglican Neo-Gothic church was built in 1885. ✎ *Map M2 • Churchillparken • 39 62 77 36 • Services 10:30am Sun & Wed • www.st-albans.dk*

8 Kongelige Afstøbningssamling
The Royal Cast Collection is heralded on the walk along the harbour with a replica of Michelangelo's statue of David. ✎ *Map M2 • Toldbodgade 40 • 33 74 85 75 • Open 2–8pm Wed, 2–5pm Sun • Free guided tours 3pm Sun (in Danish)*

9 Alexander Nevsky Kirke
This Russian orthodox church (1883) was a gift from Tsar Alexander III to celebrate his marriage to the Danish Princess Marie Dagmar. ✎ *Map L3 • Bredgade 53 • 33 13 60 46 • Open 11:30am–1:30pm*

10 Fælledparken
Copenhagen's largest park, this was once a common ground for cattle grazing and public executions. ✎ *Map D2*

Price Categories

For a three-course meal for one without alcohol, including tax (without tip).

ⓢ	up to Dkr150
ⓢⓢ	150–200
ⓢⓢⓢ	200–300
ⓢⓢⓢⓢ	300–350
ⓢⓢⓢⓢⓢ	over Dkr350

Restaurant Zeleste

🔟 Restaurants and Cafés

1 Restaurant Zeleste
 This charming restaurant with a cosy interior serves good Continental-Danish fusion food.
ⓢ Map L4 • Store Strandstræde 6 • 33 16 06 06 • www.zeleste.dk • ⓢⓢⓢ

2 Ida Davidsen
Excellent *smørrebrød* (open sandwiches – traditional Danish fare) are on offer here, with a delicious array of toppings.
ⓢ Map K3 • Store Kongensgade 70 • 33 91 36 55 • www.idadavidsen.dk • ⓢⓢⓢ

3 Salt Bar and Restaurant
Set inside an airy, 18th-century granary, this elegant bar and restaurant serves cocktails and French-Danish cuisine. ⓢ Map L3 • Toldbodgade 24–28 • 33 74 14 44 • www.saltrestaurant.dk • ⓢⓢⓢⓢⓢ

4 St Gertrud's Kloster
Housed in a medieval convent, it serves mouth-watering Danish and European dishes in a beautiful candle-lit cavern. ⓢ Map J4 • Hauser Plads 32 • 33 14 66 30 • www.sanktgertrudskloster.dk • ⓢⓢⓢⓢⓢ

5 Pussy Galore's Flying Circus
Stop at this trendy café-bar if you are in the mood for some burgers, sandwiches or salads.
ⓢ Map D3 • Skt Hans Torv 30, Nørrebro • 35 24 53 00 • www.pussy-galore.dk • ⓢ

6 Kaffesalonen
 Away from the buzz of busy streets, this cosy café sits on the peaceful banks of the Peblinge

Sø. An ideal place to enjoy a quiet meal. ⓢ Map D4 • Peblinge Dossering 6 • 35 35 12 19 • ⓢ

7 Teatime
This Rococo-style basement café offers sandwiches, cakes and sweets, and serves tea in elegant porcelain cups. ⓢ Map C3 • Birkegade 3, Nørrebro • 35 35 50 58 • Afternoon Tea 2:30pm–5pm • ⓢ

8 Bopa
Have a hearty brunch or café lunch (burgers, moussaka, etc.), and cocktails in the evening.
ⓢ Map E1 • Bopa Plads, Løgstørgade 8 • 35 43 05 66 • www.cafebopa.dk • ⓢ

9 Café Front Page
This chic, French-style café-restaurant has tasty food and great views. ⓢ Map D3 • Sortedam Dossering 21, Nørrebro • 35 37 38 27 (café); 35 37 38 29 (restaurant) • ⓢⓢⓢ

10 Kate's Joint
This popular eaterie offers cheap, good-portioned dishes with South American, Indonesian and Caribbean influences. ⓢ Map C4 • Blågårdsgade 12 • 35 37 44 96 • ⓢ

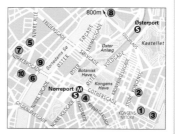

Left **2nd Birkegade** Right **Tage Andersen Boutique & Galleri**

🔟 Shopping

1 Tage Andersen Boutique & Galleri
Run by flower artist and designer Tage Andersen, this flower shop, gallery and museum is full of lovely and unique arrangements. ⬙ *Map K4 • Ny Adelgade 12 • 33 93 09 13 • www.tage-andersen.com*

2 Marie Skellingsted
Here you will find an eclectic mix of designer and vintage items, including designer wear, jewellery, bags, home accessories and kitsch items for kids. ⬙ *Map L3 • Bredgade 36 • 33 11 49 50 • www.marieskellingsted.dk*

3 House of Design
This stylish shop restores and sells high-quality, 20th-century vintage furniture, ceramics, lighting, glass and modern art. ⬙ *Map L3 • Bredgade 21 • 33 33 03 00 • www.houseofdesign.dk*

4 2nd Birkegade
Browse through a wide selection of second-hand designer wear. ⬙ *Map C3 • Birkegade 7, Nørrebro • 38 25 80 80*

5 KK Vintage
Second-hand clothes are customised to fit you and can also be personalized. ⬙ *Map C4 • Blågardsgade 31C, Nørrebro • 33 33 85 70 • www.kkvintage.dk*

6 Baan Suan
Visit this store for pretty, feminine clothing with embroidery, flower motifs and polka dots. Do also check out their varied range of colourful, ethnic jewellery, sunglasses and bags. ⬙ *Map C3 • Elmegade 18 • 35 39 19 40*

7 Nyhavns Glaspusteri
This charming glass gallery is where glassblower Christian Edwards sculpts and sells his creations. ⬙ *Map L4 • Toldbodgade 4 • 33 13 01 34 • www.copenhagenglass.dk*

8 Phenix
You will find antique pieces ranging from furniture and paintings to silverware and glass items. ⬙ *Map D3 • Ravnsborggade 16A • 35 37 55 33 • www.phenix.dk*

9 Juice
This was one of the first trendy boutiques to be set up in Nørrebro. ⬙ *Map C3 • Elmegade 17 • 35 36 15 58*

10 Glam
High-end vintage pieces are available at this second-hand store. The 1960s and 1970s collection is especially good. ⬙ *Map C3 • Silkegade 7, Nørrebro • 35 38 50 41 • www.glam.dk*

Left **Rust** Right **Gefährlich**

🔟 Nightlife

1 Props Coffee Shop
The low ceilings and relaxed ambience of this Berlin-inspired bar make it the perfect place to enjoy fine, locally brewed beer. ✆ Map C3 • Blågårdsgade 5 • 35 36 99 55

2 Gefährlich
Despite an unimpressive decor, this is one of the most popular bars in the area. It also has a good restaurant and live music. ✆ Map C3 • Fælledvej 7 • 35 24 16 00 • www.gefahrlich.dk

3 Rust
Tune into Copenhagen's alternative music scene live at this trendy bar. There is a night-club in the basement. ✆ Map C3 • Guldbergsgade 8 • 35 24 52 00 • Nightclub: Min age 21; Thu free • www.rust.dk

4 Café Pavillonen
Located beside a lake, this lovely, 18th-century-style rotunda holds open-air music perform-ances in the summer. ✆ Map D2 • Borgmester Jensens Allé 45, Østerbro • 45 83 85 87 • www.cafepavillonen.dk

5 Empire Bio Cinema
This comfortable arts cinema holds good programmes and has a cosy bar and café area. ✆ Map C3 • Guldbergsgade 29F • 35 36 00 36 • www.empirebio.dk

6 Bodega
Popular and reasonably pri-ced, this pre-clubbing venue ser-ves good bar food. It also has a dance floor; DJ sessions are held on Thursdays and Saturdays and kick in at 10pm. ✆ Map C4 • Kapelvej 1 • 35 39 07 07 • www.bodega.dk

7 Park Diskotek
This black-walled, pink-curtained club specializes in R&B and house music. Brunch is available. ✆ Map E2 • Østerbrogade 79 • 35 42 62 48 • Min age: 18–25 (Thu), over 20s (Fri), over 22s (Sat) • www.parkcafe.dk

8 Pussy Galore's Flying Circus
A hangout for Crown Prince Frederik in his bachelor days, this trendy club serves hamburgers, salads and cocktails (see p79).

9 Stengade 30
This countercultural music venue is set inside an imposing, fortress-like building, with a bar upstairs. ✆ Map C3 • Stengade 18 • 35 35 69 19 • www.stengade30.dk

10 Mexibar
This cosy, Mexican-inspired bar serves good cocktails. The staff are friendly, too. ✆ Map C3 • Elmegade 27 • 35 37 77 66

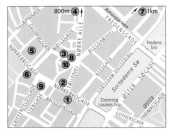

Left **Frederiksberg Slot** Right **Zoo**

Vesterbro and Frederiksberg

VESTERBRO AND FREDERIKSBERG *lie side by side to the south-west and west of the Inner City. In the 19th century both Vesterbro and Frederiksberg were outside the city walls; this was when Tivoli was built on Vesterbro's extreme edge. Until recently, Vesterbro was an area where the poor lived in humble two-room flats with no running water and included a red light district. Although the area retains an edginess not shared by the rest of Copenhagen, much of it has been regenerated. Today, you will find a thriving underground culture, designer fashion outlets and a multicultural population. In contrast, Frederiksberg was a green, prosperous country village that became increasingly popular as the upper and middle classes began to revel in the countryside in the 18th century. It is now a tranquil, upmarket residential area, and remains an independent municipality that is not officially a part of Copenhagen.*

🔟 Sights

1. Københavns Bymuseet
2. Frederiksberg Have
3. Zoologisk Have
4. SAS Radisson Royal Hotel
5. Carlsberg Museum and Visitor Centre
6. Frederiksberg Slot
7. Tycho Brahe Planetarium
8. Storm P Museet
9. Bakkehusmuseet
10. Cisternerne – Museet for Moderne Glaskunst

Storm P Museet

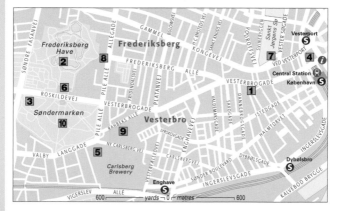

1 Københavns Bymuseet

The City Museum takes you on a journey through the city's history, right from its small beginnings on the island of Slotsholmen in the 12th century. There are many interesting exhibits, including atmospheric reconstructions, a slide show of Copenhagen through the ages and sights of a medieval town. Outside the building, don't miss the large model of medieval Copenhagen which gives you a very clear view of the buildings that existed then and the area that was covered by the city. ◈ *Map C5 • Vesterbrogade 59 • 33 21 07 72 • Open 10am–9pm Wed, 10am–4pm Thu–Mon • Adm for adults, Fri free • www.bymuseum.dk*

2 Frederiksberg Have

Frederiksberg Gardens surround Frederiksberg Slot *(see p84)* and make up a lovely green area that recalls the castle's aristocratic past. The park was designed (1798–1802) to conform with the Romantic style of the English garden. Several buildings here date back to the Golden Age (1800–50), including the Chinese Pavilion, the Neo-Classical Møstings House, the Swiss House (a cottage built especially for the royal family to have tea)

Frederiksberg Have

and the colonnaded Apis Temple. ◈ *Map A5 • Open 6am–sundown daily*

3 Zoologisk Have

Regardless of your age, the zoo makes for a lovely day out. Here you will find a variety of animals like lions, tigers, apes, monkeys (including the tiny, endangered Golden Lion Tamarins) and polar bears. ◈ *Map A5 • Roskildevej 32 • 72 20 02 00 • Open Nov–Feb 9am–4pm daily; Mar 9am–4pm Mon–Fri, 9am–5pm Sat–Sun; Apr–May, Sep 9am–5pm Mon–Fri, 9am–6pm Sat–Sun; Jun 9am–6pm daily; Jul–Aug 9am–9:30pm daily • Adm • www.zoo.dk*

4 SAS Radisson Royal Hotel

The city's tallest building, this 20-storey tower-block hotel, designed by architect Arne Jacobsen (right down to the cutlery), represents the cutting-edge design of the 1950s. About the radical design, Arne Jacobsen said, "They call it the 'punch card', and it's funny, because that is what it looks like when the windows are open on a hot summer's day." ◈ *Map G5 • Hammerichsgade 1 • 33 42 60 00 • www.radisson.com*

Københavns Bymuseet

Carlsberg Brewery

5 Carlsberg Museum and Visitor Centre

The Carlsberg Brewery, established by Jacob Jacobsen in 1847, hosts an exhibition charting the history of the brewery and its brands (including a collection of 13,000 of the 16,000 Carlsberg bottle and label designs). You can take a tour of the old, cobblestoned premises, complete with machinery, sound effects and aromas. The tour ends at the Carlsberg bar, where a couple of free beers (or soft drinks) await you. Make sure to visit the tiled Dipylon Gate (1892) and Elephant Gate (1901) at the second brewery established in 1889 by Jacob Jacobsen's son, Carl. ◈ Map A6 • Gamle Carlsberg Vej 11, Vesterbro • 33 27 13 14 • Open 10am–4pm Tue–Sun; last entry 3pm • Adm • www.visitcarlsberg.dk

6 Frederiksberg Slot

Not to be mistaken for Frederiksborg Slot in Hillerød (see p98), this castle was originally a 17th-century pavilion built by Frederik IV as a royal court. As it was rather small, it was extended several times since its construction. The building that stands here today (built in 1829) has an Italianate, Baroque architecture

and is used as a training school for army cadets. ◈ Map A5 • Not open to the public

7 Tycho Brahe Planetarium

The permanent exhibition at the Planetarium includes displays on the natural sciences, astronomy and space travel. However, one of the biggest attractions is the IMAX cinema; visitors are blown away by the enormous, high-quality images on the 1,000 sq m (over 10,500 sq ft) dome screen. Films cover topics like astronomy and space research and virtually transport you to another world. ◈ Map C5 • Gammel Kongevej 10 • 33 12 12 24 • Open 10:30am–9pm Mon–Sat, 9:30am–9pm Sun & hols • Adm • Min age for films: 3 yrs • www.tycho.dk

8 Storm P Museet

This small museum is a delightful find. It is dedicated to the whimsical and satirical wit of the Danish cartoonist Storm P, whose distinctive style seems to recall the social realism of the late 19th and early 20th centuries, such as the styles of Daumier, Toulouse Lautrec and Degas. His sense of humour comes through brilliantly in the dialogues of his characters. If you speak Danish, you will derive great enjoyment from these cartoons. However, non-Danish speakers will also enjoy the displays visually. ◈ Map A5 • Frederiksberg Runddel • 38 86 05 23 • Open May–Sep 10am–4pm daily; Oct–Apr 10am–4pm Wed, Sat & Sun • Adm for adults • www.stormp-museet.dk

9 Bakkehusmuseet

Formerly, the home of 19th-century, Golden Age literary personalities, Kamma and Lyhne Rahbek, this old house is now a cultural museum. Four rooms have retained their original decor (1802–30), and two are dedicated

If the Carlsberg Brewery has given you a taste for beer, head for Charlie's Bar, see p71; for microbreweries, see p53.

Jacob Jacobsen

Lager beer was unheard of in Copenhagen until news arrived of "Bavarian beers" being made by ageing (lagering). Jacob Jacobsen (1811–87), who made beer in the ale-making tradition, left at once for Munich to get some lager yeast. In 1847, he introduced his first lager and set up the Carlsberg Brewery (named after his son). Carlsberg lager is now among the world's best.

to the Danish poets Johannes Ewald and Adam Oehlenschläger. You will also find some HC Andersen memorabilia here. ✪ Map B6 • Rahbeks Allé 23, Frederiksberg • 33 31 43 62 • Open 11am–4pm Tue–Sun • Adm; free with Copenhagen Card • www.bakkehusmuseet.dk

10 Cisternerne – Museet for Moderne Glaskunst

This candlelit glass museum is intriguing not only for its stained glass exhibits by artists like Per Kirkeby and Robert Jacobsen, but also for its location. Set inside the cave-like water cistern of an old supply plant, it lies beneath the grassy lawns of Frederiksberg Have and has thin stalactites on the ceiling. ✪ Map A6 • Søndermarken, Roskildevej 25 • 33 21 93 10 • Open Mar–Oct 2–6pm Thu–Fri; Feb & Nov 2–5pm Mon–Fri, 11am–5pm Sat–Sun & hols • Closed Dec–Jan • Adm; free for under-14s • www.cisternerne.dk

Tycho Brahe Planetarium

A Walk Around Vesterbro

Start at the central station, Hovedbanegård, and see the *Frihedsstøtten* or "pillar of freedom" (1792). Continue down Vesterbrogade and take a left at Reventlowsgade and then a right on to Istedgade till you arrive at the old red light district. Then, walk up to **Halmtorvet**; it is now filled with cafés and restaurants. The large building directly opposite is the **Øksnehallen**, Vesterbro's biggest cultural exhibition space. Take a right on Skydebanegade, where you will see houses dating back to the 19th century. At the end of this area is a wall (1887) that protected inhabitants from shooting practice that took place in the gardens on the other side. Go through the gate in the wall, through the park, to the **Bymuseet** *(see p83)*. Take a look at the city model outside and, if you wish, visit the museum. Continue along Vesterbrogade, taking a left onto Oehlenschlægersgade, where you will find an extraordinary mosaic-covered bar that was put together by the late Nigerian-born artist, Manuel Tafat. Head back to Vesterbrogade for lunch at the **Trois Cochons** *(see p87)* on Værnedamsvej, or continue down Oehlenschlægersgade until you reach the trendy bars and boutiques on Istedgade. You could also stop over for lunch at **Café Bang & Jensen** at 130 or just enjoy a nice cup of coffee at **Riccos** at 119 *(see p86)*. Spend the rest of the afternoon browsing through the stylish shops.

Left **Designer Zoo** Right **Emmerys Bakery**

🔟 Shopping

1 Kusine Bodil og Vildbassen

This funky kids' store offers everything from Osh Kosh dungarees and Katvig denim dresses to flamingo umbrellas, toddler-sized kitchens, and retro games. ✎ Map B6 • Enghave Plads 10 • 33 24 28 84

2 Paradls

A pun on "Parad-Ice", this ice-cream parlour is famous for its range of interesting flavours, including mint-strawberry and hazelnut-mango. The chocolate range is particularly sinful. ✎ Map C5 • Vesterbrogade 47 • 35 35 79 12 • www.paradis-is.dk

3 Girlie Hurly

This shop is filled with quirky, colourful items for girls, from bags and candles to lamps and crockery. ✎ Map C6 • Istedgade 99/101 • 33 24 22 41

4 Rockahula

This intriguing little boutique is dedicated to all things Elvis. There is an especially creative line of shoes. ✎ Map C6 • Istedgade 91 • 26 23 42 67 • www.rockahula.dk

5 Gustus

You will find fabulous, reasonably priced glass items at this shop, run by a Polish glassmaker. ✎ Map C6 • Istedgade 67B • 35 83 60 68 • www.gustus.dk

6 Gallery

A lovely clothes and accessories boutique offering a mixture of new and second-hand items. Come here for old-school, street and punk styles. ✎ Map C5 • Gammel Kongevej 74

7 Designer Zoo

This is a mecca for the design-conscious, with clothing, ceramics, jewellery and even furniture by in-house designers. ✎ Map B5 • Vesterbrogade 137 • 33 24 94 93 • www.dzoo.dk

8 Emmerys Bakery

Visit this excellent gourmet store for tasty organic goodies, including breads, patisseries, chocolates, pasta, wine and cheese. ✎ Map C5 • Vesterbrogade 34 • 33 22 77 63 • www.emmerys.dk

9 Værnedamsvej

This gourmet food street has butchers, fish-mongers, wine and chocolate shops. ✎ Map C5

10 Le Marché Deli Takeaway

Stop here for good, takeaway meals. The menu varies depending on the time of day. ✎ Map C5 • Værnedamsvej 2 • www.cofoco.dk

Price Categories

For a three-course meal for one without alcohol, including tax (without tip).

⊛	up to Dkr150
⊛⊛	150–200
⊛⊛⊛	200–300
⊛⊛⊛⊛	300–350
⊛⊛⊛⊛⊛	over Dkr350

Café Lindevang

🔟 Dining

1 Café Lindevang
Café Lindevang is known for their generous portions. Meatballs and herring are accompanied by a range of *schnapps*. ✎ Map C5 • PG Ramms Allé 3 (Lindevang metro stop) • 38 34 38 34 • Closed Sun • www.cafelindevang.dk • ⊛⊛

2 Café Bang & Jensen
This ex-pharmacy is now a popular café bar. Fun cocktails and good music make for lively nights. ✎ Map C6 • Istedgade 130 • 33 25 53 18 • www.bangogjensen.dk • ⊛

3 Les Trois Cochons
Aptly named ("the three pigs" in French), this restaurant is inside an old butcher's shop. It serves great southern French food at reasonable prices. ✎ Map C5 • Værnedamsvej 10 • 33 31 70 55 • ⊛⊛⊛

4 Cofoco
Delicious, reasonably priced French-Danish food is served at a long communal table. This is a non-smoking restaurant. ✎ Map C5 • Abel Cathrins Gade 7 • 33 13 60 60 • Closed Sun • ⊛⊛⊛

5 Sticks 'n' Sushi
Try the mouthwatering sushi, sashimi or yakitori at this friendly Euro-Japanese café-bar. ✎ Map C6 • Istedgade 62 • 33 23 73 04 • www.sushi.dk • ⊛

6 Fiasco
This restaurant is famous for its delicious, rustic Italian dishes.

Enjoy a meal that rivals most gourmet food at a fair cost. ✎ Map C5 • Gammel Kongevej 176 • 33 31 74 87 • Closed Sun, Mon • www.fiasco.dk • ⊛⊛⊛

7 Gastronomique
Set inside an 18th-century building, it offers Danish cuisine served amid vases blooming with floral arrangements. ✎ Map A5 • Frederiksberg Runddel 1 • 38 34 84 36 • www.gastronomique.dk • ⊛⊛⊛⊛⊛

8 Riccos
The aroma of fresh coffee wafting from this café is hard to resist. ✎ Map C6 • Istedgade 119 • 33 31 04 40 • www.riccos.dk • ⊛

9 Formel B
Enjoy French-influenced food made with farm-fresh ingredients on the terrace or in the candlelit interiors. ✎ Map B5 • Vesterbrogade 182 • 33 25 10 66 • Closed Sun • Book ahead • www.formel-b.dk • ⊛⊛⊛⊛⊛

10 Restaurant Klubben
This pub is famous for its large portions of Danish food. ✎ Map B5 • Enghavevej 4 • 33 31 40 15 • ⊛

Left **Christiania** Right **Overgaden Neden Vandet**

Christianshavn and Holmen

AFTER THE INNER CITY, *this settlement on the island of Amager is the oldest part of Copenhagen. There are signs that have led people to believe it was inhabited during the Stone Age. In 1521, Christian II invited Dutch gardeners (whom he held in high regard) to this fertile area to plant and run market gardens. A century later, Christian IV built fortifications in the area and a town on an island at the north end. Soon, the Amagerbro bridge was built to connect the two islands; the Knippelsbro bridge stands in its place today. The canals of Christianshavn, lined with houseboats and pretty 17th-century houses, are a special attraction in this charming area that is reminiscent of Amsterdam. Holmen, to the north of Christianshavn, is made up of three man-made islets. It was created in 1690 as a naval area with*

dockyards, accommodation and offices; the navy remained here until 1989. Since then, the area has seen an increase in public spaces, forums, residential housing, and now also includes the impressive Opera House.

Operaen

🔟 Sights

1. Christiania
2. Christians Kirke
3. Vor Frelsers Kirke
4. Inderhavnen
5. Harbour Tours
6. Overgaden Neden Vandet
7. Overgaden Oven Vandet
8. Orlogs Museet
9. Operaen
10. Gammel Dok

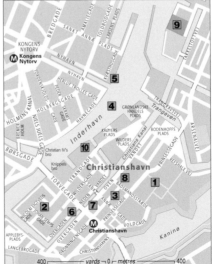

1 Christiania

In the 1970s, this rebellious squatters' enclave, set up in abandoned military barracks, was an inspirational new society with its own set of laws, readily available drugs and no tax system. The area has now become a bit more conventional; the inhabitants have been paying taxes since 1994, and the stands that sold drugs on Pusher Street closed down in 2004. However, relations between Christiania and the Danish authorities have ne-ver been friendly and the area's status is still in doubt. There are no actual sights but many hippy hangouts. ⊗ Map M5

2 Christians Kirke

Originally known as Frederiks Kirke, this interesting, yellow-brick church was renamed as Christians Kirke (after Christian IV, founder of this part of Copenhagen) in 1901. It was built between 1755–59 in the Rococo style by Nicolai Eigtved, Frederik V's master architect. The interior looks almost like a theatre, with second-level seating galleries and the altar taking the place of the stage. The elegant tower was added by Eigtved's son-in-law, GD Anthon, 10 years after the church was built. ⊗ Map K6 • Strandgade 1 • 32 54 15 76 • Open Mar–Oct 8am–6pm daily; Nov–Feb 8am–5pm daily

3 Vor Frelsers Kirke

This magnificent Baroque church was built (1682–96) by the Dutch-Norwegian architect Lambert van Haven in the form of a Greek cross. Its trademark twisted tower was added 50 years later (1749–52). Inside the church is bright and well-lit, thanks to its white walls and large windows. Look out for the

Christians Kirke

putti-covered font, presented in 1702 by Frederik IV's morganatic wife who hoped to have children. Unfortunately, she died in 1704 during childbirth and the baby died nine months later. Don't miss the marvellous altarpiece which represents God as the Sun and depicts the scene in the garden of Gethsemane, when Christ prayed that he should not die on the cross. The organ, built like a three-storey house, rests on two elephants. ⊗ Map L6 • Sankt Annae Gade 29 • 32 54 68 83 • Open Apr–Aug 11am–4:30pm Mon–Sat, noon–4:30pm Sun; Sep–Mar 11am–3:30pm Mon–Sat, noon–3:30pm Sun (tower presently closed for repairs; due to reopen in April 2009) • Adm for tower • www.vorfrelserskirke.dk

4 Inderhavnen

You simply cannot ignore the water in Christianshavn. Its canals are tributaries of the Inner Harbour (Inderhavnen), which separates it from the rest of the city. The harbour widens further up the coast to become the Sound (Øresund). ⊗ Map J6–M4

Orlogsmuseet

5 Harbour Tours

A harbour tour, which usually starts from the harbour end of Nyhavn *(see p8)*, is a great way to see Copenhagen. It will take you through the canals of Christianshavn; from the water, you can appreciate the maritime nature of the city. You will also get a sense of how it developed over the centuries. The quay-sides, built in the 17th century, are now studded with small boats and houseboats moored alongside. ◈ *Map L4*

6 Overgaden Neden Vandet

Overgaden Neden Vandet (which means "upper street below the water") is the quayside that runs along the Sound side of the Christianshavn canal. The street is lined with buildings, including the Michelin-starred restaurant, Era Ora *(see p93)*, dating back to the 17th century when the canal was first built. ◈ *Map L6*

7 Overgaden Oven Vandet

Opposite Overgaden Neden Vandet is its counterpart, Overgaden Oven Vandet (which means "upper street above the water"). As on the other side, it has cobbled streets and is lined with 17th-century houses. You will also find the Royal Danish Naval Museum here *(see below)*. ◈ *Map L6–M5*

8 Orlogsmuseet

The Royal Danish Naval Museum, located in the area that was influenced by the navy and its docks for centuries, documents Danish naval history from 1669. It is choc-a-bloc with beautiful, detailed models of ships and harbours, as well as a few reconstructions of important Danish sea battles. Some of the models were used as sailors' teaching aids for cadets, showing them how to strip and re-rig the sails. Most of the information is available in both Danish and English. The museum building (dating back to 1781) was originally used as a naval hospital and then as a state prison until the 1830s. ◈ *Map L5 • Overgaden Oven Vandet 58 • 33 11 60 37 • Open noon–4pm Tue–Sun • Adm for adults; Wed free • www.orlogsmuseet.dk*

9 Operaen

The Opera House is the first major public building to be built in the Holmen area since the navy vacated the docks in 1979. Architect Henning Larsen emphasized its location near the water with large glass windows and no pillars on the ground floor. The interior has a maritime feel as well, with balconies, open spaces and white railings. The position of the Opera House caused much controversy when it was built, especially in relation to the Amalienborg, which lies directly opposite it on the other side of the Sound. The design of the Opera House was also the cause of a little bit of friction when its benefactor, industrialist Mærsk McKinney Møller, insisted that his own architectural ideas also be incorporated into the construction *(see p8)*.

🔟 Gammel Dok

Gammel Dok (which means "Old Dock") was built in 1739, a time when the navy's ships moored alongside. The warehouse dates back to 1882 and now houses the Danish Architecture Centre. It holds exhibitions and provides a working space for young artists and architects who win scholarships to study here. A café on the first floor offers great views over the water. ◈ *Map L5 • Dansk Arkitektur Centre, Strandgade 27B • 32 57 19 30 • Open 10am–5pm • Adm for adults • www.dac.dk*

Harbour Tour

Walking Tour

Morning

🕐 Start at the Knippelsbro Bridge by the **Børsen** *(see p36)*. Built in 1937, the bridge takes its name from Hans Knip, the tollkeeper of the first bridge built here in the 17th century. Turn right to visit **Christians Kirke** on Strandgade *(see p89)*. Then, retrace your steps and cross Torvegade, walking right up to the corner of Sankt Annæ Gade. At the corner is No 32 (built in 1622–24), said to be the oldest house in Christianshavn. Turn right and then left on to **Overgaden Oven Vandet** and walk along the canal. Pop inside the **Royal Danish Naval Museum** for a quick visit. If you are curious about **Christiania** *(see p89)*, take a right down Brobergsgade, cross Prinsessegade and head to Pusher Street. If you are not going to the opera in the evening, continue along the canalside and take a right turn at Bodenhoffs Plads, then a left onto Værftsbroen. Keep walking (or take the bus 66) towards the **Opera House**. Hop on a Harbour bus back to Knippelsbro for lunch at **Café Wilder** *(see p93)* on Wildersgade and head down Sankt Annæ Gade to visit **Vor Frelsers Kirke** *(see p89)*.

Afternoon

🍷 Spend the afternoon shopping. If you are in the mood for a drink, there are cafés along the Christianshavns Kanal. Linger over supper at L'Altro on **Torvegade** *(see p92)* or catch a performance at the **Opera House** *(see p8)* (taking the bus 66 or the water bus from Knippelsbro).

Left **Skosalonen** Right **In Blik**

🔟 Shopping

1 PaGode Design
Oriental-style, natural-fibre women's clothing are available here. They also have a good collection of stylish bags, shoes, boots, sandals, leggings and coats. ✆ *Map L5 • Overgaden Oven Vandet 90 • 32 96 00 34*

2 Shop Bit Antik
This tiny shop is filled with pieces from Denmark's yester-years. Among the antiques, furni-ture and knick-knacks are old dolls and doll houses, books, glasses, sculpture and porcelain. ✆ *Map L6 • Prinsessegade 17B • 32 54 09 62 • www.bitantik.com*

3 Porte à Gauche
This trendy boutique offers Scandinavian designer wear for women. You will also find classic, exotic Julie Sandlau jewellery. ✆ *Map L5 • Torvegade 20 • 32 54 01 40 • www.porteagauche.dk*

4 Skosalonen
Right next to Porte à Gauche is its sister shoe store. Equally chic, it offers a superb collection of designer brands for men and women. ✆ *Map L5 • Torvegade 16 • 32 52 01 40 • www.skosalonen.dk*

5 In Blik
This delightful gift shop has an eclectic collection, including stylish lighters and gadgets, shoes and jewellery, children's games, snow globes and unusual photo frames. ✆ *Map L5 • Torvegade 38 • 32 57 65 61*

6 Lagkagehuset Bakery
Well known for its breads, cakes and pastries, they have a particularly fine selection of goodies during Christmas. ✆ *Map L6 • Torvegade 45 • 32 57 36 07 • Open Sun*

7 Ginnungagab
Visit this store for clothes, woollens and skins from the Arctic region. ✆ *Map K6 • Overgaden Oven Vandet 4A • 32 54 22 11*

8 Hilbert København
Jewellery at this shop, run by goldsmith Morten Hilbert, is made to order. ✆ *Map L6 • Sankt Annæ Gade 24 • 33 93 53 01*

9 Medusa
Despite its scary name, this is the perfect place for cute toys for kids. ✆ *Map L6 • Torvegade 33*

10 Yo-Yo
Owned by former supermodel Helena Christensen's mother, it sells clothes and accessories the family no longer needs. ✆ *Map L6 • Sankt Annæ Gade 31 • 20 46 31 81*

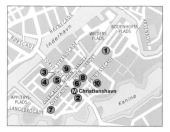

Price Categories

For a three-course meal for one without alcohol, including tax (without tip).

Ⓚ	up to Dkr150
ⓀⓀ	150–200
ⓀⓀⓀ	200–300
ⓀⓀⓀⓀ	300–350
ⓀⓀⓀⓀⓀ	over Dkr350

Sofiekælderen

⁉️🔟 Cafés, Bars and Restaurants

1 Era Ora
One of the best Italian restaurants in Denmark, Era Ora offers warm service in a tranquil setting. There is a changing set menu with delicious courses and 90,000 bottles of Italian vintage wine. Ⓜ *Map L6 • Overgaden Neden Vandet 33B • 32 54 06 93 • Closed Sun • www.era-ora.dk • ⓀⓀⓀⓀⓀ*

2 L'Altro
Relish homely Umbrian-Tuscan dishes in the relaxed atmosphere of this *antiristorante*, a 1950s Italian expression that means "to dine at home". Ⓜ *Map L6 • Torvegade 62 • 32 54 54 06 • Closed Sun • www.laltro.dk • ⓀⓀⓀⓀ*

3 Spicy Kitchen Cafe
This cosy Indian-Pakistani restaurant is a big hit with the locals. Ⓜ *Map L6 • Torvegade 56 • 32 95 28 29 • Ⓚ*

4 Grisobasovitz
Popular chef Søren Gericke's charming restaurant serves delicious, traditional Danish dishes. Ⓜ *Map L6 • Overgaden Neden Vandet 17 • 32 54 54 08 • Closed Mon • ⓀⓀⓀⓀ*

5 Sofiekælderen
This popular, though rather spartan, café-bar is so close to the water, you could climb down to the boats moored alongside. Enjoy a night out at its famous bar and night-club. Ⓜ *Map L6 • Overgaden Oven Vandet 32 • 32 57 77 01 • Ⓚ*

6 Café Wilder
Enjoy good French-Italian-inspired food and coffee at this café. Ⓜ *Map L5 • Wildersgade 56 • 32 54 71 83 • www.cafewilder.dk • Ⓚ*

7 Noma
This restaurant serves great Nordic cuisine made with fresh ingredients. Ⓜ *Map M5 • Strandgade 93 • 32 96 32 97 • www.noma.dk • ⓀⓀⓀⓀ*

8 Rabes Have
Opened for local soldiers and sailors in 1632, this is the oldest pub in Copenhagen. Ⓜ *Map K6 • Langebrogade 8 • 32 57 34 17 • Closed Mon • Ⓚ*

9 Bastionen & Løven
Famous for its large brunch, this is also a pretty spot for a romantic evening. Ⓜ *Map L6 • Christianshavns Voldgade 50 • 32 95 09 40 • www.bastionen-loven.dk • ⓀⓀⓀⓀ*

10 Oven Vande Café
Enjoy tasty salads, soups and paninis at this café. Ⓜ *Map L5 • Overgaden Oven Vandet 44 • 32 95 96 02 • www.cafeovenvande.dk • Ⓚ*

Left **Experimentarium** Right **Helsingør**

Beyond Copenhagen

ALTHOUGH COPENHAGEN ITSELF *will easily keep you entertained for several days, the area around the city offers many opportunities for days out. Roskilde and Helsingør provide a taste of Nordic history, right from the Viking era to the founding of Copenhagen. Get a sense of medieval maritime defense of the Sound at Helsingør's Kronborg Slot and explore the royal lifestyle in the 17th and 18th centuries at Frederiksborg and Charlottenlund. Art and literature lovers can drop in at Arken, Louisiana, Ordrupgaard and the Karen Blixen Museum, home to internationally-acclaimed collections. The Experimentarium and the Akvarium are a must-visit for kids.*

Frederiksborg Slot

Charlottenlund Slotshave

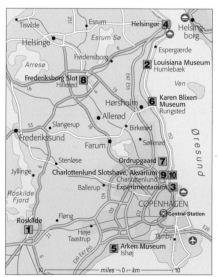

🔟 Sights

1. Roskilde
2. Louisiana Museum
3. Experimentarium
4. Helsingør
5. Arken Museum for Moderne Kunst
6. Karen Blixen Museum
7. Ordrupgaard
8. Frederiksborg Slot
9. Charlottenlund Slotshave
10. Akvarium

Preceding pages: **Interior of Den Sorte Diamant.**

Roskilde

Roskilde, a mere 25 minutes away from the city centre by train, makes for a fascinating day out. Older than Copenhagen itself, this was the original seat for Absalon, Bishop of Roskilde and founder of the city. Here you will find a medieval cathedral, a royal burial site and the wonderful Viking Ship Museum, which holds shipwrights' workshops (see p100).

Louisiana Museum

This should be high on the list for modern art enthusiasts. The museum houses an impressive selection of works by international artists like Picasso, Alberto Giacometti and Francis Bacon, and Danish masters like Asger Jorn and Per Kirkeby. There is also a children's wing here, which offers art-related activities for kids between 3 and 16 years (call for details). The seaside location, lovely garden and excellent café make the museum even more appealing.
⊗ Map B1 • Gammel Strandvej 13, Humlebæk • 49 10 07 19 • Open 11am–10pm Tue–Fri, 11am–6pm Sat–Sun • Adm for adults; free for under-18s, free with Copenhagen Card • Guided tours available in English: book ahead • Dis access • www.louisiana.dk

Roskilde

Experimentarium

This fun and educational science centre has over 300 interactive experiments that relate to the human body and the world we live in. See how your loudest shout compares to the roar of a lion; try to solve a giant 3D puzzle of the human body; or crawl barefoot through the Sensation Zone. Younger kids are encouraged to explore concepts of sound and magnetism in a special pavilion. ⊗ Map B2 • Tuborg Havnevej 7, Hellerup • 39 27 33 33 • Open 9:30am–7pm Mon–Fri (to 9pm Tue), 11am–5pm Sat–Sun & hols • Adm charges; free for 0–2 year olds • Dis access • www.experimentarium.dk

Helsingør

In the 1400s, this harbour town levied tax on all sea traffic that passed through the Sound, which is just 4 km (2.5 miles) wide at this point – the town name translates as "Penny Sound". Apart from a pretty medieval centre, other sights include the 16th-century castle, Kronborg Slot, the Carmelite monastery and the Teknisk Museum of planes, trains and automobiles (see p102).

Café in Louisiana Museum

5 Arken Museum for Moderne Kunst

This wonderful museum houses a rotating permanent collection of contemporary international and Danish art, along with temporary exhibitions. The white, ship-like museum building, designed by Danish architect Søren Lund, is like an exhibit in itself. It offers great views of the sand dunes and the sea at Køge Bugt. ◈ Map B3 • Skovvej 100, Ishøj • 43 54 02 22; Special tours: 43 57 34 55 • Open 10am–5pm Tue, Thu–Sun; 10am–9pm Wed • Adm; free with Copenhagen Card • www.arken.dk

6 Karen Blixen Museum

Anyone who has read the novel *Out of Africa* will find this museum, home of author Karen Blixen (pen name: Isak Dinesen), fascinating. Born here in 1885, Blixen returned in 1931 after the death of her lover, Denys Finch Hatton. The house is exactly as it was when she lived here. You can see the furniture she brought back from Nairobi, including Hatton's favourite chair. The museum holds exhibitions of her paintings and drawings, letters, a slide show of her life in Africa, readings by Blixen herself and a lovely garden with a bird sanctuary. You can also visit her grave at the foot of

Ewald's Hill. ◈ Map B2 • Rungsted-lund, Rungsted Strandvej 111, Rungsted Kyst • 45 57 10 57 • Open May–Sep 10am–5pm Tue-Sun; Oct–Apr 1pm–4pm Wed–Fri, 11am–4pm Sat–Sun • Adm; free for under-14s, free with Copenhagen Card • Book ahead for guided tours in foreign languages • www.karen-blixen.dk

7 Ordrupgaard

This art gallery houses a superb collection of French Impressionist art and interesting works by 19th- and 20th-century Danish artists. The building is a delightful, 19th-century mansion. ◈ Map B2 • Vilvordevej 110, Charlotten-lund • 39 64 11 83 • Open 1pm–5pm Tue, Thu–Fri, 10am–6pm Wed, 11am–5pm Sat–Sun • Adm; free for under-18s, free with Copenhagen Card • Free audio guide • Book ahead for guided tours in foreign languages • www.ordrupgaard.dk

8 Frederiksborg Slot

Built in 1560 by the architect king, Christian IV, this copper-turreted, fairy-tale castle stands next to a lake and is surrounded by gardens. The interior is a pleasing mix of Renaissance and Rococo decor. After a fire in 1859, the castle was rescued from ruin by JC Jacobsen (of Carlsberg fame), who founded a national history museum here. Be

Karen Blixen Museum

Danmarks Akvarium

sure to visit the beautiful chapel.
⊗ Map B1 • DK-3400 Hillerød • 48 26
04 39 • Open Apr–Oct 10am–5pm; Nov–
Mar 11am–3pm • Baroque Gardens Oct–
Mar 8am–6pm daily; Apr–Sep 8am–9pm
daily • Adm; free with Copenhagen Card
• www.frederiksborgmuseet.dk

9 Charlottenlund Slotshave
The lovely park around
Charlottenlund Palace, is a
16-minute train ride from the
city centre. Redesigned in
the Romantic English style
in the 19th-century, the park's
attractions include a charming
thatched cottage, once lodgings
for the Royal Life Guards. The
French Renaissance chateau-
style palace is closed to the
public. ⊗ Map B2 • www.ses.dk

10 Danmarks Akvarium
Over 285 marine species
from the world over are housed
in over 70 aquariums at this
museum. Everything from
piranhas to turtles of all sizes
(some the size of your little
finger) are found here. One of
the "residents" is said to have
swum to the North Sea coast all
the way from the Mediterranean
Sea. ⊗ Map B2 • Kavalergården 1,
Charlottenlund • 39 62 32 83 • Open
10am–5pm • Adm • www.akvarium.dk

Day Tour

Morning

Start your day by hopping
onto a train at Hoved-
banegården and heading
to **Helsingør**. Visit the
castle at Helsingør before
lunch, and then wander
around the old town (see
pp97 and 102). Alter-
natively, get off the train
at **Humlebæk** and visit the
Louisiana Museum (see
p97). If at Helsingør, have
an open sandwich and a
beer at one of the many
pubs at the town square;
if in Louisiana, have lunch
at the garden café.

Afternoon

After lunch, if you are in
Helsingør, wander through
the medieval streets,
especially **Strandgade** and
Stengade (see p102). Visit
the medieval **Domkirke**,
the **Teknisk Museum**
and the **Bymuseum**
(see p102), housed in
a Carmelite monastery
dating back to 1516. If in
Louisiana, return to the
station and take a train to
Rungsted Kyst and drop
in at the **Karen Blixen
Museum**; try one of the
homemade cakes at the
café. Or get off the train at
Klampenborg to see the
fascinating Impressionist
paintings at **Ordrupgaard.**
If you are at Helsingør or
the **Karen Blixen Museum**,
start heading back towards
Copenhagen in the early
evening, stopping at
Klampenborg for an
evening of entertainment
at the **Bakken Fun Fair**.
You can also catch a bite
to eat here. If you are at
Ordrupgaard, visit the café
and then walk to the fun
fair; either cut through the
park or use the main road.
On Wednesdays, you can
wander around Louisiana
till 9pm.

Left **Vikingeskibsmuseet** Centre **Roskilde Kloster** Right **Hestetorvet**

TOP 10 Roskilde

1 Roskilde Domkirke
This magnificent cathedral holds the remains of 39 Danish monarchs. ✪ Map P6 • Domkirkestræde 10 • 46 35 16 24 • Open Apr–Sep 9am–5pm Mon–Sat, 12:30–5pm Sun; Oct–Mar 10am–4pm Tue–Sat, 12:30–4pm Sun • Adm; free for under-7s and with Copenhagen Card • www.roskildedomkirke.dk

2 Stændertorvet
This small square in front of the Town Hall has been a market place since the Middle Ages. ✪ Map P6 • Markets on Wed & Sat

3 Roskilde Slot
Built in 1733–36 for royal visitors, this Baroque palace houses the Museum of Contemporary Art, the Palace Wing, and Palace Collections gallery. ✪ Map P6 • Stændertorvet 3 • Museum: 46 36 88 74, Open 11am–5pm Tue–Fri, noon–4pm Sat & Sun; Palace Wing: 46 32 14 70, Open mid-May–mid-Sep 11am–4pm daily; Palace Collections: 46 35 78 80, Open 11am–4pm daily, closed 24, 25, 31 Dec, 1 Jan • Adm for adults • www.ses.dk

4 Roskilde Museum
This museum illustrates Roskilde's history from the time when it was Denmark's first capital. ✪ Map P5 • Sankt Ols Gade 15–18 • 46 31 65 00 • Open 11am–4pm daily, closed 24, 25, 31 Dec & 1 Jan • Adm for adults; free with Copenhagen Card • www.roskildemuseum.dk

5 Roskilde Kloster
This manor was bought in 1699 by two aristocratic women who converted it into a home for unmarried mothers. ✪ Map P6 • Sankt Pederstraede 8 • 46 35 02 19 • www.roskildekloster.dk

6 Kirkegård
Now a park, this medieval churchyard holds the graves of many prominent Roskilde citizens. ✪ Map Q6

7 Hestetorvet
The Horse Market is set in what was Roskilde's largest square for centuries. Look out for the three giant vases that commemorate Roskilde's millennium in 1998. ✪ Map Q6

8 Vikingeskibsmuseet
The popular Viking Ship Museum displays five 1,000-year-old Viking vessels that were recovered from the watery depths in 1962: a warship, longship, ferry and deep sea vessel. Viking-ship boat trips are available in the summer (see below). ✪ Map P4 • Vindeboder 12 • 46 30 02 00 • Open 10am–5pm daily • Adm for adults; free for under-17s • www.vikingeskibsmuseet.dk

9 Viking Ship Trips
Sail for 50 minutes in a replica of a 1,000-year-old Viking warship. ✪ Map P4 • Vikingeskibsmuseet, Vindeboder 12 • 46 30 02 53 • www.vikingeskibsmuseet.dk

10 Skomagergade & Algade
The city's two main, beautifully paved streets, are lined with shops and cafés. ✪ Map P6

Roskilde is home to one of the largest open air music festivals in Europe, usually the first week in July (www.roskilde-festival.dk).

Left **Eyes (1997)** at the museum's entrance Right **Two Piece Reclining Figure No. 5 1963–64**

🔟 Louisiana Museum

1 Big Thumb 1968
This striking, 2-m (6-ft) tall bronze thumb is modelled after the thumb of its creator, French sculptor César Baldaccini (1921–98).

2 Dead Drunk Danes 1960
Rebel artist Asger Jorn (1914–1973) was awarded the Guggenheim International Award for this expressive abstract painting. However, he rejected the accolade and sent Harry Guggenheim an infuriated telegram: "Go to hell with your money bastard *stop* Never asked for it *stop* Against all decency to mix artist against his will in your publicity *stop*".

3 People and the Seal 1949
This fantastical painting is by Carl Henning Pedersen (1913–07), a member of the abstract expressionist CoBrA group.

4 Marilyn Monroe 1967
American artist Andy Warhol (1928–1987) created a series of famous silkscreen prints of Marilyn Monroe using Pop Art colours. This is one of them.

5 Déjeuner sur l'Herbe (1961)
Painted by Pablo Picasso (1881–1973), this abstract work pays homage to Edouard Manet's revolutionary painting of 1862–63, in which a nude woman sits in a classical setting, having a picnic with two fully clothed modern men.

6 Alberto Giacometti Collection
The museum owns an impressive collection of 13 sculptures and several drawings by Alberto Giacometti (1901–66). The elongated figures with rough textures are reminiscent of African sculpture.

7 Two Piece Reclining Figure No. 5 1963–64
This bronze work by Henry Moore (1898–1986) occupies a beautiful spot between the trees, its humanoid, organic forms melding with the landscape.

8 Homage to the Yellow Square: Climate 1962
This is part of the series titled *Homage to the Square* by Josef Albers (1888–1976), the influential Bauhaus artist who explored the chromatic relationship of different coloured flat squares.

9 Figures in a Landscape (1977)
In this painting by Roy Lichtenstein (1923–97), an exponent of Pop Art, symbols and images are broken down in a Cubist style and set in a surreal landscape.

10 Garden and Views
The museum's gardens and views are as much a part of its charm as its exhibits. Here, the visual arts, architecture and landscapes exist in unity; the sculptures create silhouettes against the sky, and the gardens enhance the sculptures' appeal.

Left **Marienlyst Slot** Right **Axeltorv**

⟳10 Helsingør

1 Kronborg Slot
Famous as the setting of Shakespeare's play *Hamlet*, this castle was first built in 1420. Its Great Hall is the largest in Europe. ◈ *Map Q2 • Kronborg 2C • 49 21 30 78 • Open May–Sep 10:30am–5pm daily; Oct 11am–4pm Tue–Sun; Nov–Mar 11am–3pm Tue–Sun • Adm • www.kronborgslot.dk*

2 Danmarks Teknisk Museum
Explore an impressive collection of machines here, including steam engines, cars (one dating back to 1888) and a variety of aeroplanes. ◈ *Fabriksvej 25 • 49 22 26 11 • Open 10am–5pm Tue–Sun • Adm; free with Copenhagen Card • www.tekniskmuseum.dk*

3 Festivals
In summer, Helsingør hosts a number of festivals, including the Maritime Festival, Sunset Jazz Festival and Shakespeare's plays. ◈ *www.visithelsingor.dk*

4 Karmeliterklosteret
Built in the 15th century, this Gothic-style monastery belonged to the Carmelite Order. ◈ *Map P2 • Sankt Annæ Gade 38 • 49 21 17 74 • Open mid-May–mid-Sep 10am–3pm daily, mid-Sep–mid-May 10am–2pm daily • Adm • www.sctmariae.dk*

5 Helsingør Bymuseum
Next door to the Carmelite Monastery, the Town Museum was originally used as a hospital for sailors. It now houses interesting displays that recall the building's original function as the Karmeliterklosteret's infirmary. ◈ *Map P2 • Sankt Annagade 36 • 49 28 18 00 • noon – 4pm daily • www.helsingor.dk/museum*

6 Axeltorv
This main square features a statue of Erik of Pomerania, the Polish prince who ruled Denmark from 1397–1439. ◈ *Map P2*

7 Stengade & Strandgade
Stengade is a pedestrianized street in the medieval quarter. Some houses on Strandgade date back to 1459. ◈ *Map P3*

8 Sankt Olai Domkirke
Note the 15th-century crucifix, the 1568 Renaissance pulpit and the carved wooden altar. ◈ *Map P2 • Sankt Annæ Gade 12 • 49 21 04 43 • Open May–Aug 10am–4pm Mon–Sat, Sep–Apr 10am–2pm daily • www.helsingordomkirke.dk*

9 Marienlyst Slot
Named after Frederik V's wife Juliana Maria, this Neo-Classical manor is now a museum. Its elegant 18th-century interiors are well preserved. ◈ *Map N1 • Marienlyst Allé 32 • 49 28 18 30 • Currently closed for renovation • Adm for adults; free with Copenhagen Card*

10 Øresundakvariet
This sea-water aquarium has a variety of tropical fish and Baltic species. ◈ *Map P1 • Strandpromenaden 5 • 35 32 19 70 • Open Jun–Aug 10am–5pm daily; Sep–May noon–4pm Mon–Fri • Adm for adults; free with Copenhagen Card*

For information on the season of Shakespeare's plays performed each August at Kronborg Castle, visit www.hamletsommer.dk.

Price Categories

For a three-course meal for one without alcohol, including tax (without tip).

⊛	up to Dkr150
⊛⊛	150–200
⊛⊛⊛	200–300
⊛⊛⊛⊛	300–350
⊛⊛⊛⊛⊛	over Dkr350

Søstrene Olsen

🔟 Places To Eat

1 Skovriderkroen

This brasserie restaurant across Charlottenlund's sandy beach, turns into a lively nightspot by sunset. *Map B2 • Strandvejen 235, Charlottenlund • 39 46 07 00 • www.skovriderkroen.dk • ⊛⊛⊛*

2 Sletten Kro

Visit this cheerful, traditional inn for delicious modern Danish cuisine and a splendid view over the harbour. *Map B2 • Gammel Strandvej 137, Humlebæk • 49 19 13 21 • ⊛⊛⊛⊛*

3 Restaurant Jacobsen

Dine in style on the famous Arne Jacobsen chairs, and even use Jacobsen cutlery. The menu spans modern Italian, French and Danish cuisine. Fish is especially good. *Map B2 • Strandvejen 449, Klampenborg • 39 63 43 22 • www.restaurantjacobsen.dk • ⊛⊛⊛⊛*

4 Den Gule Cottage

Set in an idyllic location, this small, timber-framed restaurant was created in 1844 by architect Bindesbøll. The dishes are prepared with fresh, seasonal ingredients. *Map B2 • Strandvejen 506, Klampenborg • 39 64 06 91 • www.dengulecottage.dk • ⊛⊛⊛⊛⊛*

5 Mikkelgaard

This lovely restaurant, set on a farm with lawns rolling down to the sea, serves good Danish food. *Map B2 • Rungsted Strandvej 302, Hørsholm • 45 76 63 13 • www.mikkelgaard.dk • ⊛⊛⊛⊛*

6 Restaurant Gilleleje Havn

Enjoy traditional Danish seafood at this fine old seamen's inn (1895) on the harbour. After the meal, stroll along the beautiful sandy beach. *Map A1 • Havnevej 14, Gilleleje • 48 30 30 39 • www.gillelejehavn.dk • ⊛⊛⊛*

7 Nokken

This smart, seaside restaurant serves modern Mediterranean dishes with a Danish twist and transforms into a popular nightspot after dark. *Map B2 • Rungsted Havn 44, Rungsted • 45 57 13 14 • www.nokken.dk • ⊛⊛⊛⊛⊛*

8 Røgeriet Rungsted

Try the popular smoked fish served at this old smokery. *Map B2 • Rungsted Havn 22, Rungsted • 45 76 06 08 • www.roegeriet.com • ⊛⊛⊛⊛⊛*

9 Jan Hurtigkarl & Co.

This cosmopolitan restaurant is the brainchild of the innovative chef, Jan Hurtigkarl. Have a meal on the seafront terrace and look out for Hurtigkarl's ingenious, pyramid-shaped wood burning barbecue. *Map B1 • Nordre Strandvej 154, Ålsegård • 49 70 90 03 • www.hurtigkarl.dk • ⊛⊛⊛⊛⊛*

10 Søstrene Olsen

The food at this cosy cottage-style restaurant is delicious. The seafood is particularly good. *Map B1 • Øresundsvej 10, Hornbæk • 49 70 05 50 • www.sostreneolsen.dk • ⊛⊛⊛⊛⊛*

STREETSMART

COPENHAGEN'S TOP 10

Left **An SAS plane** Right **International ferry**

📖10 Getting There and Around

1 Arriving By Air
Airlines that serve Copenhagen directly are Scandanavian Air lines (SAS), Aer Lingus, British Airways and Mærsk Air. The airport is 12 km (7 miles) away from the city; it takes about 15 mins to get to the city by train, or 45 mins by bus (both cost the same). You will also find a taxi rank just outside the airport (terminal 3).

2 Arriving By Train
International trains run to and from many European cities, including Hamburg and Berlin. All international trains stop at Hovedbanegården, the city's main station.

3 Arriving By Road
If driving into Copenhagen from Sweden, you can take the Øresund bridge from Malmø. If driving in from Germany and crossing the island of Funen, you can take the Great Belt Bridge to Sjælland, the island on which Copenhagen is situated. Both bridges exact a toll.

4 Arriving By Ferry
You can take a DFDS Seaways ferry to Copenhagen from Poland (Swinoujscie) or Norway (Oslo). Ferries from the UK (Harwich) stop at Esbjerg; from here, you can take a train to Copenhagen or drive 300 km (186 miles) on the E20 motorway.

5 Local Public Transport
The bus, local (S) train and metro systems are frequent and efficient. In Greater Copenhagen, you can use a single ticket or discount clip card to transfer between these three systems. These cards are available for 10 journeys and work out cheaper than the basic tickets available. ⊗ www.dsb.dk/english

6 Harbour Buses
Harbour buses (901 and 902) run the length of the harbour between Den Sorte Diamant and Gefionspringvandet. ⊗ Daily 6am–6pm/7pm, every 10 mins.

7 Taxis & Rickshaws
Taxis have a FRI (free) sign on the roof. You can pay by credit card and also get receipts. Catch the cycle rickshaws for short rides at Storkespringvandet, Tivoli, Rådhuspladsen and Nyhavn.

8 Driving & Parking
You can drive if you are over 18 and hold a valid licence. Always carry the registration papers and reflecting triangle. Parkering forbudt means no parking within certain time limits. Motoring offences attract on-the-spot fines.

9 Bicycles
Bicycles offer a great way to enjoy more of Copenhagen in a short period of time. There are cycle paths throughout the city. Free city bikes are available from mid-April to mid-December at 110 special stands around the city.

10 On Foot
Copenhagen is a lovely place to walk around. As it is relatively small, many of the sites are a short walk away from each other, unless you plan on heading out to Nørrebro or crossing town. Tourist signposting is helpful.

Directory

Copenhagen Airport
• 32 31 32 31
• www.cph.dk

DSB Train Tickets Reservation and Info
• 70 13 14 15
• www.dsb.dk

DFDS Seaways (Ferries)
• Copenhagen: 33 42 30 00
• Oslo: 33 42 30 00
• Polferries (Swinoujscie): 33 13 52 23
• www.dfdsseaways.dk

Car Hire
• Budget Rent A Car: 33 55 05 00
• Europcar: 70 11 66 99; www.europcar.dk

Bicycle Information
• Kobenhavn Cykler: www.rentabike.dk
• City Cykler: www.citycykler.dk

Left **Airport information board** Centre **Tourist information sign** Right **Wonderful Copenhagen**

🔟 General Information

1 Best Time to Visit

Summertime is ideal since you can enjoy as many as 16–18 hours of daylight on clear days. Christmas is also fun, with fairy lights and celebrations at Tivoli, the open-air ice rink at Kongens Nytorv and plenty of markets, concerts and other entertainment. There is plenty for kids to do on other Danish school holidays as well: week 7, July to mid-August, and week 42. The only time you might want to avoid, due to chilly winds and the limited hours of daylight (only seven), is Dec–Jan.

2 Visas

European Union citizens do not require a visa to enter Denmark and can stay for up to 90 days. Others should check whether their country has reciprocal agreements on waiving visa requirements. Foreign nationals who wish to work in Copenhagen must have a work and residence permit for paid or unpaid work. ✎ *www.nyidanmark.dk/ en-us/coming_to_dk/ coming_to_dk.htm*

3 Duty Free Goods & Customs

Denmark imposes a limit on what can be brought into the country. Do not carry food articles that are not vacuum-packed by the manufacturer. Articles in commercial quantities and presents valued at more than 1,350kr are subject to customs duty. US citizens are liable to pay duty if carrying goods worth more than $400. Many shops offer tax-free shopping for non-EU visitors for a minimum purchase of 300kr; remember to collect a Global Refund Tax Free Cheque from the store, so you can apply for a 13–19 per cent refund. ✎ *www. globalrefund.com*

4 Tourist Information

The Wonderful Copenhagen tourist office (situated just opposite the main station) offers a variety of brochures and lets you book hotels. To receive free tourist information on your mobile, text "woco" to 1231 (mobile charges apply). ✎ *Wonderful Copenhagen: 70 22 24 42, www.visitcopenhagen.dk*

5 Opening Hours

Opening hours for shops are: Mon–Thu 9:30am/10am–5:30pm, Fri 9:30am/10am–7pm/8pm; Sat 9:30am/10am–noon/1pm (to 5pm on the first Saturday of the month). Weekend hours may be extended in tourist areas, especially in summer. Museums are closed on Mondays.

6 Weekly Listings

The Copenhagen Post (each Friday) provides a useful guide to events taking place in the city. Danish speakers can check the Friday guide sections of Politiken and Berlingske.

7 Websites

Tourist board websites provide useful information. Other websites are listed below. ✎ *www. visitcopenhagen.com* • *www.visitdenmark.dk* • *www.aok.dk/section/ english*

8 Public Holidays

Public holidays include New Year's Day, Maundy Thursday, Good Friday, Easter Monday, Common Prayer's Day, Ascension Day, Whit Monday and Christmas.

9 Admission Prices

Some museums are always free, others are mostly free on Wednesdays. The Copenhagen Card offers discounts and allows entry to 60 attractions and museums.

10 For Children

Several museums have children's facilities, and most restaurants provide high chairs – some even have special children's menus (call to check). Hotels like the Admiral and DGI-Byen also offer babysitting services. The airport has play areas, baby-changing facilities and buggies.

Left **A typical pharmacy** Right **Police van**

Health and Security

1 Health Insurance & Precautions

Although emergency medical treatment is free, make sure you have suitable travel insurance. EU nationals should bring their European Health Insurance cards. Visitors from Schengen countries (several EU countries plus Iceland, Norway and Switzerland) can carry up to 30 days' supply of prescribed medication; others must carry no more than 14 days' supply. Documents stating the need for the medication may be required.

2 Pharmacies

Pharmacies have a green sign saying "A" (*Apotek*). Prescription medication can only be bought at pharmacies. Credit cards are not accepted; full payment is required. ✎ *Steno Apotek, Vesterbrogade 6C (opp. main station)*

3 Medical Treatment

Tourists are covered by public health services as per the agreement between Denmark and their home country. Emergency hospital treatment is free for all tourists, unless the medical facility determines that the emergency occurred as a result of a pre-existing condition. Refunds for doctor's fees can be obtained from the nearest municipal or health insurance office before leaving Denmark.

4 Personal Safety

Copenhagen is a safe city, but visitors must take precautions. Make sure your bags are closed securely and your credit cards, mobile and money are kept in a safe place. Also, avoid carrying large amounts of cash. If you are a victim of a crime, contact the police *(see below)* immediately.

5 Police

To file reports, contact the nearest police station *(see Directory)*. In a crisis, call the emergency services number.

6 Dental Treatment

Head to Dentist Tandlægevagten (Oslo Plads 14, tel. 35 38 02 51), open 8am–9:30pm Mon–Fri, 10am–noon Sat–Sun. Be prepared to pay at least 150kr on the spot.

7 Doctors & Hospitals

Outside office hours, call either Doctor On Call or 24-hour Doctor Watch. If an emergency arises, go to the Accident and Emergency section of any hospital *(see Directory)*.

8 Theft

Report theft at a police station *(see Directory)* at once; you will be issued a crime report note, which you will need for insurance claims.

9 Disabled Access

Wonderful Copenhagen, or WoCo *(see p107)*, has a list of places that offer facilities for the disabled. For wheelchair information, contact DSB Handicap *(see Directory)*.

10 Lost Property

For items lost on the bus, call 36 13 14 15; for items lost on local (S)-train: 36 14 17 01. Lost property office: 38 74 88 22.

Directory

Pharmacies
• *Steno Apotek (24 hrs): 33 14 82 66*

Police
• *Station City: Halmtorvet 20; 33 25 14 48*
• *Politivagten: Copenhagen Central Station; 33 15 38 01*
• *Slotsherrensvej (lost and found): 38 74 88 22*

Emergency Services
112

Doctors & Hospitals
• *Doctor On Call: 70 13 00 41*
• *24-hour Doctor Watch: 38 88 60 41*
• *Amager Hospital: 32 34 35 00* • *Bispebjerg Hospital: 35 31 23 73* • *Frederiksberg Hospital: 38 16 35 13*
• *Rigshospitalet: 33 45 35 45*

Handicap Services
• *DSB Handicap Service: 70 13 14 19*
• *4 x 35 Taxi (book ahead): 35 39 35 35*
• *Woco List: www.visitcopenhagen.com/composite-253.htm*

Left **Danish currency** Centre **ATM machine** Right **A Danish letterbox**

🔟 Banking and Communications

1 Local Currency
Danish notes come in denominations of 1,000 kr, 500 kr, 200 kr, 100 kr and 50 kr. Coins come in 20 kr, 10 kr, 5 kr, 2 kr, 1 kr, 50 øre (half a krone) and 25 øre.

2 Banks & ATMs
Banks are usually open Mon–Wed 10am–10pm; Thu 10am–6pm. Most ATMs are open 24 hours a day, and are usually found outside banks and metro stations. The most popular card is Visa, but finding machines that accept MasterCard or American Express shouldn't be a problem, either.

3 Exchange
There are many exchange bureaux throughout the city. Those open for the longest include Den Danske Bank´s exchange office (6am–10pm) at Copenhagen Airport, and the Forex (8am–9pm) at the Hovedbånegard station. Hotels have foreign exchange services, but the rate is lower than at banks or exchange bureaux.

4 Credit Cards
International credit cards are not always accepted, especially at small outlets. There may also be an extra charge if you pay by credit card. If you lose your credit card, call your credit card company immediately *(see Directory)*.

5 Post Offices
Post offices are usually open Mon–Fri 9am/10am–5.30pm; Sat 9am–noon (or closed). You can arrange for a Poste Restante service at any post office. International mail arrives faster with the Faste Deliver A-mail or Prioritaire mail service. 🔗 *www.postdanmark.dk*

6 Telephones
The international dialling code for Denmark is +45; there are no area codes. To make international calls from Denmark, first dial 00. Public telephones accept coins and pre-paid phone cards. Insert 5–20 kr for international calls; however, you will not receive change. You cannot make collect calls to the US from public phones. For information and directory assistance, call 113.

7 Mobiles
GSM compatible mobile phones will work. There are three main ser-vice providers *(see Directory)*. Roaming is expensive, so check your service provider's rates for calls from abroad.

8 Internet
There are many internet cafés in the city. Boomtown Netcafé is one of the biggest, with 108 computers. Use It *(see p107)* lets you surf, but you can't make print outs. Most hotels offer internet access, too.

9 TV & Radio
Cable and satellite TV provide easy access to channels in English and other languages. Radio Denmark International (1062 Mz) broadcasts news in English at 10:30 am, 5:05pm and 10pm.

10 Newspapers & Magazines
Denmark's national newspapers include: *Borsen*, *Ekstra Bladet*, *Jyllands-Posten*, *Information* and *Politiken*. For local news in English, get the *Copenhagen Post* (free). You can find most major UK and US newspapers at kiosks.

Directory

Credit Card Companies
• *AMEX and Master-Card: 44 89 27 50*
• *Visa and Other cards: 44 89 29 29*
• *Danish PBS 24-hr hotline (for other credit cards): 44 89 29 29*
• *Diners Club: 36 73 73 73*

Mobile Companies
• *Sonofon: 80 29 29 29*
• *TDC-Mobil: 80 80 80 20*
• *Telia: 80 40 40 40*

Internet Cafés
• *Boomtown Netcafé: Axeltorv 1–3*
• *Faraos Cigarer: Skindergade 27*
• *Nethulen: 1st floor, Istedgade, 114*

Left **Traffic lights at a pedestrian crossing** Right **Jaywalking**

🔟 Things To Avoid

1 Jaywalking
The Danes never jay-walk, even if there is no traffic in either direction. If you can't resist the urge to do so, don't be surprised if a grumpy po-liceman decides to arrest you for breaking the law. Always cross at the pedestrian crossing when the signal turns green. For the benefit of the visually impaired, a beeping sound is emitted for the entire duration when it is safe to cross.

2 Exceeding the Speed Limit or Drinking & Driving
Exceeding the speed limit is illegal and you can be fined on the spot. If you don't pay, your car may be impounded. Drinking and driving is strictly prohibited as well. Do not drive if the level of alcohol content in your blood is more than 0.5 (two drinks). For alcohol levels of up to 1.2, a large fine is imposed. If the level is 1.2–2, you could lose your license. Levels above 2 may re-sult in a prison sentence of two weeks or more.

3 Buying Drugs
Buying and selling drugs in Denmark is illegal, just as in most other places, and the penalties are severe. Earlier, buying drugs from a booth on Pusher Street in Christiania was almost *de rigueur* for young visitors. However, Pusher Street has now been shut down and drugs cannot be bought openly.

4 Forgetting to Clip Tickets on Public Transport
Always remember to clip your ticket to validate it when you travel on public transport. Clipping mach-ines can be found on buses and on platforms of train and metro sta-tions. If you do not clip your ticket, you can be fined by inspectors.

5 Visiting Museums on Monday Without Checking
Most museums are shut on Mondays, though a few are closed on Tues-days instead. So, check in advance for frustration-free sightseeing.

6 Stepping Out in Front of a Bike
Visitors who are not used to having cycle lanes in their cities might mistake this area for part of the pavement. However, bikes have right of way here. Remember to treat cycle lanes as you would the rest of the road.

7 Grumbling in English
Practically everyone be-low the age of 70 (and many above) speak excellent English, as they have been watching English and American films and TV for long. So, if you grumble in English, everyone from the bus driver up will know exactly what you are saying.

8 Praising the Swedes
The Danes and their neighbours, the Swedes, have been at loggerheads for centuries. These days, the Danes continue to be rude about the Swedes, but in a tongue-in-cheek way. However, they often do mean it when they say that the Swedes travel to Copenhagen only to buy alcohol, as it is less expensive here.

9 Insulting the Royal Family
The Danes are very respectful of their royal family, especially the present queen. Insulting them is highly inadvis-able; it would be similar to (if not a little worse) insulting someone's favourite sports team. However unintentional it may be, it could damage your relations with your hosts – especially the older generation.

10 Not Making Eye Contact When "Skolling" a Drink
It is considered rude if you don't lock your gaze with your drinking partner when you raise a toast and say "*Skål*". This tradition of "skolling" dates back to the Vikings, who used to chop off the heads of vanquished enemy chiefs and drink out of their skulls.

Left **Café in Vesterbro** Right **Gardens of the Royal Library**

🔟 Copenhagen on a Budget

1 Reservations
Make your hotel reservations well in advance to get the best deals. The peak season is usually Apr/May–Sept/Oct. Online hotel prices are often cheaper, but it is a good idea to ring the hotel and ask about their best prices and deals.

2 Sights
A well-planned trip can be surprisingly inexpensive. Walking the streets is free and also fascinating. Discount clip cards (see p106) reduce your expense on public transport. Parks and gardens (except Tivoli) are free, and often host free entertainment, especially in the summer. Several state-run museums are free; others are free on Wednesdays or Sundays. The Danish National Theatre sells unsold tickets at half price after 4pm on the day of the performance. ✆ Danish National Theatre box office: Tordenskjoldsgade 7

3 Sightseeing Passes
The Copenhagen Card supplied by the Danish Tourist board is a good investment, offering lots of great discounts for sightseeing and transport. For information, or to buy the Copenhagen Card in advance (minimum of 10 days), visit the Wonderful Copenhagen website (see p107).

4 Cheap Eats
As in most other places, pizza and pasta dishes are cheap in Copenhagen. Fast food outlets are plentiful, and you can get a sandwich or a burger and chips for under 50 kr. If you want something more substantial for under 150 kr, a main course, bread and a glass of wine or beer in a café will easily fit your budget. Some restaurants, especially Thai, offer reasonably priced buffet lunches.

5 Hotel Breakfasts
Although breakfast is a modest affair for most Danes, visitors are spoiled for choice at hotels. Eat-all-you-want breakfasts offer good value for money, even at 100–150 kr – especially if you can fill up for the day. Some hotels include breakfast in the price of the room, so check when you book.

6 Meals
Lunch (Frokost) is served from noon–2pm. Supper (Aftensmad) is usually served from 6pm–9:30pm/10pm, although you can call to check if the kitchen is open after that. Supper often costs more, but you are served larger portions. Late night snacks are limited to hot dogs or kebabs from a stall.

7 Tipping
Tips are usually included in bills at restaurants and hotels, so it is not considered rude if you don't leave one. In cheaper places, rounding the bill up is perfectly acceptable. In more expensive restaurants, it is customary to leave a tip, but it can be as little as 5 per cent of the bill. You don't have to tip taxi drivers.

8 Free Music Events
Every Wednesday in the spring and summer, students from the Royal Danish Academy of Music perform classical concerts at the Theatre Museum. Look out for the street bands at the summertime jazz festival (see p43) and for Friday Rock at Tivoli (see p11). ✆ www.onsdags koncerter.dk ✆ www.jazzfestival.dk

9 Other Free Events
During Christmas, special markets are held with some shops like the Royal Copenhagen (see p68), putting up exhibitions. Free skating is on offer at rinks at Kongens Nytorv, Frederiksberg Runddel and Blågårds Plads. Museums conduct free workshops for kids (closed 24–25 Dec).

10 Movies
Some cinemas offer lower rates from Mon–Thu before 6pm (ring to check). Between Jul–Aug, free open-air screenings are held by Zulu Sommerbio and Fri Film. ✆ www.zulu.dk

Left **The Square** Right **Palace Hotel**

🔟 Luxury Hotels

1 Palace Hotel
Overlooking Rådhus-pladsen, this old-fashioned Victorian hotel is currently undergoing major renovation. By 2007, its traditional English-style decor will be blended with a fresh, modern design. ◈ Map H5 • Rådhuspladsen 47 • 33 14 40 50; Booking: 33 42 85 21• www.palace-hotel.dk • ⊗⊗⊗⊗⊗

2 Hotel d'Angleterre
Olden day grandeur meets modern luxury at this 250-year-old hotel. It has a plush palm court, banquet rooms, a spa and a great restaurant serving international cuisine. ◈ Map K4 • Kongens Nytorv 34 • 33 12 00 95 • www.dangleterre.dk • ⊗⊗⊗⊗⊗

3 Sofitel Plaza
Built in 1913, this hotel has spacious rooms and traditional decor. The Library Bar, full of 18th-century books, is one of the best bars in the city. ◈ Map G5 • Bernstorffs-gade 4 • 33 14 92 62 • www.sofitel.com • ⊗⊗⊗⊗

4 FRONT
This modern, child-friendly boutique hotel offers rooms of various sizes. Each room has been individually deco-rated and enhanced with attractive artwork. ◈ Map L4 • Skt Annæ Plads 21 • 33 13 34 00 • www.front.dk • ⊗⊗⊗⊗

5 Sankt Petri
One of Copenhagen's coolest 5-star hotels, every room is delightfully decorated with orchids and abstract art and the bathrooms are luxurious. It has a lively glass-roofed atrium featuring international DJs, as well as a popular cocktail bar. ◈ Map H4 • Krystalgade 22 • 33 45 91 00 • www.hotelsktpetri.com • ⊗⊗⊗⊗

6 Axel Guldsmeden
Part of the Guldsmeden group, this former budget hotel is set to open in 2007. Plans are on to equip it with a wellness centre and pool. ◈ Map G6 • Helgolands-gade 7–11 • 33 31 32 66 • www.hotelguldsmeden.dk • ⊗⊗⊗⊗

7 Nyhavn 71
This cosy 4-star hotel at the end of Nyhavn was once a warehouse built to store goods from ships on the harbour. The area is very peaceful and does not suffer from noisy tourists; few wander this far down the quayside. The restaurant offers a substantial breakfast. ◈ Map L4 • Nyhavn 71 • 33 43 62 00 • www. 71nyhavnhotel.com • ⊗⊗⊗⊗

8 Phoenix
Owned by the famous Arp-Hansen group, this comfortable 4-star hotel, just off Kongens Nytorv, is decorated in a French, Louis XIV style with contemporary colour and touch. Housed in a 17th-century building that originally belonged to an aristocratic family called Von Plessen, the hotel has a restaurant and 'English pub'-style bar. ◈ Map L3 • Bredgade 37 • 33 95 95 00 • www.phoenixcopenhagen.dk • ⊗⊗⊗⊗

9 The Square
This modern 3-star hotel opposite the Palace Hotel stands on the Town Hall square. It is replete with stylish pony-hair chairs placed at the entrance and groovy Arne Jacobsen chairs in the reception area. The rooms are comfortable and the breakfast on offer excellent. ◈ Map H5 • Rådhuspladsen 14 • 33 38 12 00 • www.thesquare.com • ⊗⊗⊗

10 Grand Hotel
A short walk down Vesterbrogade, this 4-star hotel is located in a lively city area. In the summer, you can sit in its pave-ment café and enjoy a spot of people-watching over coffee. The rooms are spacious and the decor traditional without being ornate. The hotel's Restaurant Frascati is very good and serves some tasty Italian cuisine. ◈ Map G5 • Vesterbrogade 9 • 33 27 69 00 • www.grand hotelcopenhagen.com • ⊗⊗⊗

Price Categories

For a standard, double room per night (with breakfast if included), taxes and extra charges.

⊕ up to Dkr1,000
⊕⊕ 1,000–1,400
⊕⊕⊕ 1,400–1,800
⊕⊕⊕⊕ 1,800–2,200
⊕⊕⊕⊕⊕ over Dkr2,200

Bertrams Hotel Guldsmeden

🔟 Expensive Hotels

1 Comfort Hotel Esplanaden
This is Denmark's first non-smoking hotel. Situated close to the Amalienborg, it is housed inside an 19th-century building. The hotel was refurbished in 2000. ◎ Map L2 • Bredgade 78 • 33 48 10 00 • www. choice hotels.dk • ⊕⊕⊕

2 Hotel Alexandra
More than a century old, this excellent 3-star hotel became popular in the last decade for its original, 20th-century furniture design classics ranging from Kaare Klint chairs to Akademi chandeliers designed by Poul Henningsen. There are three non-smoking floors and allergy-tested rooms. ◎ Map G5 • HC Andersen Boulevard 8 • 33 74 44 44 • www.hotel-alexandra.dk • ⊕⊕⊕

3 Imperial Hotel
Stylish and welcoming, the decor is based on modern Danish design principles. You will also find an entire floor dedicated to the work of the Danish designer Børge Mogensen. ◎ Map G5 • Vester Farmimagsgade 9 • 33 12 80 00 • www. imperialhotel.dk • ⊕⊕⊕

4 Opera
This 3-star Arp-Hansen hotel is set in a building that dates back to 1869; the hotel opened here only in the 1950s. The decor is

modern with traditional English overtones, such as Regency-striped armchairs. A "Wall of Fame" shows the famous people who have visited the hotel in the last 50 years. ◎ Map K4 • Tordenskjoldsgade 15 • 33 47 83 00 • www. hotelopera.dk • ⊕⊕⊕

5 Hilton Copen-hagen Airport
Live in style at this posh 5-star hotel, equipped with a pool, gym, three restaurants and bars and some good business facilities. The decor is distinctly Scandinavian with plenty of light wood. It was voted the best ho-tel in Denmark in 2005. ◎ Ellehammersvej, 20 Kastrup • 32 50 15 01 • www.hilton.dk • ⊕⊕⊕

6 Kong Arthur
Close to Rosenborg Slot (see pp20–21), this 4-star hotel exudes a certain old-world charm, with a dash of chintz. It has reasonably big rooms and a conservatory-style breakfast room. ◎ Map G3 • Nørre Søgade 11 • 33 11 12 12 • www.brochner-hotels.dk • ⊕⊕⊕

7 Bertrams Hotel Guldsmeden
This 3-star hotel is unlike any other in Copenhagen and has a delightful ethnic decor, displaying pottery from Mexico, furniture from Indonesia and carpets from Pakistan. It serves

delicious breakfasts from Emmerys (see p86). ◎ Map B5 • Vesterbrogade 107 • 33 25 04 05 • www. hotelguldsmeden.dk • ⊕⊕⊕

8 Hotel Kong Frederik
There have been inns and hotels on the site since the 14th century, but this hotel dates back to 1868. Services include a hair salon, florist and internet access. ◎ Map H4 • Vester Voldgade 25 • 33 12 59 02 • www. nphotels.dk • ⊕⊕⊕

9 SAS Radisson Scandinavia
With 542 rooms and suites, this is Denmark's biggest hotel. Standing tall in Christianshavn, it offers great views and world-class services. There are four restau-rants, including the child-friendly Mamas and Papas. ◎ Map J6 • Amager Boulevard 70 • 33 96 50 00 • www. radissonsas.com • ⊕⊕

10 SAS Radisson Falconer
Smaller than the other two Radisson hotels in the city, this bright and airy hotel offers a wide range of services and conveniences. It is primarily aimed at business travellers and even has a conference centre next door. ◎ Map B4 • Falkoner Allé 9 • 38 15 80 01 • www.radissonsas. com • ⊕⊕⊕

Left **Danmark** Right **Hotel Fox**

🔟 Mid-Range Hotels

1 Guldsmeden Carlton
This lovely hotel is about halfway down Vesterbrogade. Sophisticated yet relaxed, it has an ethnic decor with dark-wood furniture, white-washed walls and Egyptian cotton sheets. It offers delicious organic breakfasts. The staff are very helpful and some even let you hire their bikes. The hotel is a short distance away from the main station. 🅂 *Map C5 • Vesterbrogade 66 • 33 22 15 00 • www. hotelguldsmeden.dk •* ⓚⓚ

2 Clarion Collection Mayfair
Close to the city's main attractions, this comfortable hotel is furnished mainly in an English style with a hint of the oriental. 🅂 *Map G6 • Helgolandsgade 3 • 70 12 17 00 • www. choicehotels.dk •* ⓚⓚ

3 Danmark
This contemporary 3-star hotel is set inside an 18th-century building. It offers babysitting services and free internet access. Look out for good web weekend deals. 🅂 *Map H5 • Vester Voldgade 89 • 33 11 48 06 • www.hotel-danmark.dk •* ⓚⓚ

4 Comfort Hotel Østerport
This modern hotel is a short walk away from Kastellet *(see p78)* and the Little Mermaid *(see p9)*. It provides facilities such as babysitting, internet access and a recreational game room. 🅂 *Map K1 • Oslo Plads 5 • 70 12 46 46 • www. choicehotels.dk •* ⓚⓚ

5 Ibsens Hotel
All rooms are non-smoking and individually decorated in this friendly hotel. It has a beautiful courtyard and offers good facilities. 🅂 *Map G3 • Vendersgade 23 • 33 13 19 13 • www.ibsenshotel. dk •* ⓚⓚ

6 Hotel Fox
Check out the rooms in this cool, quirky hotel. Each has been decorated by a different designer and reflects a different mood. It also has a good restaurant-café and live music from Thursday to Saturday. 🅂 *Map G4 • Jarmers Plads 3 • 33 13 30 00 • www.hotelfox.dk •* ⓚⓚ

7 Christian IV
Ideally located away from the busy city centre, this 3-star hotel is a stone's throw away from Kongens Have and Rosenborg Slot *(see pp20–21)*. There are a range of great free services on offer, including coffee or tea and snacks served through the day and entry to the gym on Adelsgade. Check for the best prices. 🅂 *Map K3 • Dronningens Tværgade 45 • 33 32 10 44 • www. hotelchristianiv.dk •* ⓚⓚ

8 Hotel Absalon
Fairly standard, this hotel offers some good services, including free internet access in the lobby and trouser presses. The decor, though not exceptional, varies from floor to floor. Rooms are reasonably-sized, but verge on the chintzy. They do not have air conditioning. 🅂 *Map G6 • Helgolandsgade 15 • 33 24 22 11 or 33 31 43 44 (bookings) • www. absalon-hotel.dk •* ⓚⓚ

9 First Hotel Vesterbro
This fabulous 4-star hotel has a good location on Vesterbrogade. It has large, attractive rooms with minimalist decor. There is a wonderful atrium with potted trees where you can catch a bite to eat. Interestingly, in the seedier days of Vesterbro, it was the local porn cinema. 🅂 *Map C5 • Vesterbrogade 23–29 • 33 78 80 00 • www.firsthotels. dk/vesterbro •* ⓚⓚ

10 Best Western Hotel Hebron
Conveniently located in the city centre, this hotel offers good-sized rooms with modern decor. There is free internet access in the rooms and access to facilities like room safes. The lounge, with its free hot drinks, is a good place to relax. 🅂 *Map G6 • Helgolandsgade 4 • 33 31 69 06 • www.hebron.dk •* ⓚⓚ

Hotel Absalon

Price Categories

For a standard, double room per night (with breakfast if included), taxes and extra charges.	
ⓦ	up to Dkr1,000
ⓦⓦ	1,000–1,400
ⓦⓦⓦ	1,400–1,800
ⓦⓦⓦⓦ	1,800–2,200
ⓦⓦⓦⓦⓦ	over Dkr2,200

🔟 Budget Hotels

1 Selandia

If you are looking for an inexpensive place to spend the night, opt for this purely functional hotel. It is centrally located and only a couple of streets from the main station. ❧ Map G6 • Helgolandsgade 12 • 33 31 46 10 • www.hotel-selandia.dk • ⓦ

2 Norlandia Star Hotel

Recently refurbished by the Norlandia group, this is another centrally located hotel. It is a reasonably-priced option for the traveller on a budget. ❧ Map G6 • Colb-jørnsensgade 13 • 33 22 11 00 • www.norlandiahotels.dk/star • ⓦ

3 Hotel Cosmopole

This is a central, functional hotel with some spacious rooms. Located close to a nightclub, it can get a little too noisy for some visitors. ❧ Map G6 • Colbjørnsensgade 5–11 • 33 21 33 33 • www.accorhotel.dk • ⓦ

4 Copenhagen Crown

Acquired and updated by the Profil-Hotel group, this is a good budget option. ❧ Map C5 • Vesterbrogade 41 • 33 21 21 66 • www.profilhotels.com • ⓦⓦ

5 Absalon Annex

A 1-star annex of Hotel Absalon, this offers clean and practical rooms with colour TVs and sinks. There are shared showers and toilets on each floor. You have free internet access and the buffet breakfast is included in the price of the room. ❧ Map G6 • Helgolandsgade 15 • 33 24 22 11 • www.absalon-hotel.dk • ⓦ

6 Cab Inn City

A five-minute walk from Tivoli, this is the newest and largest Cab Inn in the city. Based on the idea of a ship's cabin, the rooms are small but perfectly designed with all the modern conveniences tucked into a clever storage design. You can pick from bunk beds in twin rooms, double rooms and family rooms. The hotel has a pleasant ambience and offers good buffet breakfasts. ❧ Map H6 • City Mitchellsgade 14 • 33 46 16 16 • Dis access • www.cab-inn.dk • ⓦ

7 Cab Inn Copenhagen Express

This 3-star hotel in the popular chain is just a 12-minute walk from Rådhuspladsen, situated on the other side of the reservoirs. If you walk down the road and look across the water, you will be able to see the Tycho Brahe Planetarium (see p84). ❧ Map C4 • Danasvej 32, Frederiksberg • 33 21 04 00 • www.cab-inn.dk • ⓦ

8 Cab Inn Scandinavia

Just a block away from the Cab Inn Copenhagen Express and a road before the Peblinge Sø, this Cab Inn hotel is equipped with all the modern conveniences at the other two Cab Inns in the city. ❧ Map C4 • Vodroffsvej 55, Frederiksberg • 35 36 11 11 • www.cab-inn.dk • ⓦ

9 DGI-Byen

Just behind the central station, the DGI-Byen has a good sports and swimming centre (see p45), making it a great place to stay for families. Modern, comfortable and clean, it has an Ikea-esque, Danish design. The price of the room includes breakfast, one free entrance to the spa and free entry to the hotel's swimming centre. ❧ Map G6 • Tietgensgade 65 • 33 29 80 50 • www.dgi-byen.dk/hotel • ⓦ

10 Hotel Centrum

This recently renovated 3-star hotel is part of the DGI-Byen group. One of the perks of staying at this hotel is that guests are allowed free entry to the DGI-Byen swimming centre and spa, which is located only a short walk away from the hotel (see p45). ❧ Map G6 • Helgolandsgade 14 • 33 31 31 11 • www.dgi-byen.com/hotel • ⓦⓦ

Left **Dansk Bed and Breakfast** Centre **Sleep In Fact** Right **YMCA Interpoint**

Other Accommodation

1 Danhostel Amager
Four kilometres from the city centre (20 mins by bus), this renovated hostel offers rooms with 2–5 beds, a kitchen, laundry services, internet access, a TV room, lockers and a children's playground. It is very close to a large shopping mall known as Fields. An IAH Card is a requirement. ◈ *Vejlandsallé 200, Sundbyvester • 32 52 29 08 • Open 2 Jan–15 Dec; Check-in: 1pm–5pm • Dis access • www.copenhagen youthhostel.dk • ®*

2 Sleep In Fact
This sports centre which was a former factory, stays open during the summer as a hostel. The dormitories have 30–40 beds and a kitchen. You also have access to some useful facilities, including the internet, a safe deposit, storage space, bike rental and sport facilities. It is a 10–15 minute walk from the main train station. ◈ *Map C5 • Valdemarsgade 14, Vesterbro • Open 26 Jun–30 Aug; Reception: 7am–12pm & 3pm–3am • www.sleep-in-fact.dk • ®*

3 Sleep In Green
Run by the young set in trendy Nørrebro, this hostel has an eco-friendly outlook (hence "In Green"). It uses only organic and recyclable materials and is also into electricity and water conservation. A good place to meet other travellers. ◈ *Map D3 • Ravnsborggade 18, Nørrebro • 35 37 77 77 • Open end-May–end-Oct; Reception: 4pm–noon • www. sleep-in-green.dk • ®*

4 YMCA Interpoint
Open only for a short time in the summer, this small hostel (36 beds) is very popular. It is set inside an old house and has a large living room with a piano. The rooms, though small, offer a good garden view and free internet access. ◈ *Map C5 • Valdemarsgade 15, Vesterbro • 33 31 15 74 • Open Jul–mid-Aug • www.ymca-interpoint.dk • ®*

5 City Camp
Centrally located and close to the harbour, this is a good option if you want to park your camper van or caravan while in the city. To make reservations via e-mail *(see below)*, provide them your license plate number and your arrival and departure dates. ◈ *Fisketorvet / Vasbygade, Vesterbro • 21 42 53 84 • Open 1 Jun–1 Sep • Reservations@citycamp. dk • www.citycamp.dk • ®*

6 Bellahøj Camping
If you wish to pitch a tent, this is the nearest campsite to town. It is in a residential area, 4.5km from the centre on the 2A bus or a short bike ride. It provides all the basic amenities that are required while camping. ◈ *Hvidkildevej 66 • 38 10 11 50 • Open 1 Jun–31 Aug • www. bellahoj-camping.dk • ®*

7 Adina Apartment Hotel
Slightly away from the city centre, this apartment hotel offers great facilities, including a gym, babysitting services, an indoor heated pool, flat screen TVs and CD players. ◈ *Amerika Plads 7 • 39 69 10 00 • www.adina.eu.com • ®®*

8 Citilet
These smart hotel suites in the city centre are tastefully decorated. Breakfast is included in the price of the room. ◈ *Map K4 • Fortunstræde 4 • 70 22 21 29 • www. citilet.dk/english • ®®®*

9 Dansk Bed & Breakfast
This B&B agency offers good quality private accommodation in central locations. ◈ *Map G4 • Sankt Peders Stræde 41 • 39 61 04 05 • www.bbdk. dk • ®*

10 The Hospitality Club
Stay for free and meet a global network of hosts, travellers and locals who aim to increase intercultural understanding. ◈ *www. hospitalityclub.org*

Left **Admiral** Centre **Marriott Copenhagen**

🔟 Rooms With A View

1 SAS Radisson Royal Hotel

This famous Radisson hotel, designed by Arne Jacobsen in the 1950s, is packed with 5-star comforts. The rooms afford great views over the city. On the 20th floor, the well-known Alberto K restaurant serves a fusion of Nordic and Italian cuisine (see p83). ⓢ ⓦⓦⓦ

2 Copenhagen Island

This state-of-the-art hotel is on an island in the middle of Copenhagen harbour. Architect Kim Utzon's extraordinary building places a great emphasis on the play of glass and light. The rooms offer scenic views of the Sound and is cheaper on weekends. ⓢ Map J6 • Kalvebod Brygge 53 • 33 38 96 00 • www.copenhagen islandhotel.com • ⓦⓦⓦ

3 Copenhagen Strand

This 3-star hotel is tucked away on a pretty, quiet street opposite the Christianshavn canal. The decor is rustic and the view is wonderful. It is cheaper on weekends. ⓢ Map L4 • Havnegade 37 • 33 48 99 00 • www.copenhagenstrand.com • ⓦⓦⓦ

4 Admiral

Originally an 18th-century granary, the rooms in this splendid 4-star hotel overlook the Sound and offer a stunning view of the Opera House (see p8). Two cannons guard the entrance and the foyer displays some beautiful models of ships. The rooms are very comfortable and the restaurant, Salt, is excellent. ⓢ Map L3 • Toldbodgade 24–28 • 33 74 14 14 • www.admiralhotel.dk • ⓦⓦⓦ

5 Marriott Copenhagen

Reasonably priced for a 5-star hotel, it has a lovely reception atrium and attractive rooms. Views of the Sound are spectacular; the rooms on the 10th and 11th floor are especially recommended. ⓢ Map J6 • Kalvebod Brygge 5 • 88 33 99 00 • www.marriott.com • ⓦⓦⓦ

6 Scandic Copenhagen

Standing tall near the Tycho Brahe Planetarium (see p84), it offers magnificent panoramic views over Copenhagen's rooftops. Try out their fabulous breakfasts. For the best rates, check the "Early" and "Flex" deals. ⓢ Map C5 • Vester Søgade 6 • 33 14 35 35 • www.scandic-hotels.com/copenhagen • ⓦⓦⓦ

7 Danhostel Copenhagen City

This new 5-star Danhostel is one of the biggest in the city. It is located close to Tivoli and Rådhuspladsen and offers great views over the city's attractions. ⓢ Map C5 • HC Andersen Blvd 50 • 33 11 85 85 • Dis access • www.danhostel.dk/copenhagencity • ⓦ

8 Skovshoved Hotel

Away from the bustle of central Copenhagen, this peaceful seaside hotel is over 350 years old. Tastefully decorated in a Scandinavian style, it is surrounded by fishermen's houses and offers beautiful views. ⓢ Map B2 • Strandvejen 267, Charlottenlund • 39 64 00 28 • www.skovshovedhotel.dk • ⓦⓦⓦ

9 Skodsborg Kurhotel and Spa

Formerly a summer palace, this badehotel (bathing hotel) is over a century old. Overlooking the sea, it is the perfect destination for health and fitness fanatics, offering a range of therapies and fitness programs. ⓢ Skosborg Strandvej 139, Skodsborg • 45 58 58 00 • www.skodsborg.dk/uk • ⓦⓦⓦⓦ

10 Dragør Badehotel

This 3-star harbour hotel in the fishing village of Dragør is a popular destination with tourists and boasts rooms with gorgeous views of the sea and the countryside. ⓢ Drogdensvej 43, Dragør • 32 53 05 00 • www.badehotellet.dk • ⓦ

General Index

Acknowledgements

The Author
Antonia Cunningham would like to thank the following for their help and support while researching and writing this book:
Henrik Thierlein at Wonderful Copenhagen, Annette Wæber of Meet the Danes and Bodil and Troels Joergensen and their family for their kind hospitality; Hotel Square, No 71, Admiral Hotel, Bertrams Hotel Guldmedsen; Annette Larsen, Caroline Disum and Louise Albeck at Café Rabes Have; Mads Grimstad and Nina Wengel at the Opera House and Brian at Barcelona for their helpful advice; Nicolaj Steen Møller for his comments and advice; and all the staff who kindly showed me around hotels and restaurants and provided information. I would also especially like to thank Nick Simpson, Susan Hazledine, my sister Francesca Mitchell and my editor Fay Franklin, who was very understanding of my pregnant state and the odd delay that went with it.

Photographer Jon Spaull

Fact checking and additional text Nikolaj Steen Møller, Laura Pilgaard Rasmussen

AT DORLING KINDERSLEY

Publisher Douglas Amrine

Publishing Manager Scarlett O'Hara

Design Manager Karen Constanti

Senior Cartographic Designer Casper Morris

Senior Editor Fay Franklin

Project Editor Alastair Laing

DTP Designer Natasha Lu

DK Picture Library Romaine Werblow, Rose Horridge

Senior Picture Researchers Taiyaba Khatoon, Ellen Root

Picture Researchers Sumita Khatwan, Rhiannon Furbeari

Production Linda Dare

AT CREATIVE QUOTIENT (A Repro Enterprise)

Art Director Asha Madhavan

Editors Shantala Bellare, Gauri Kelkar

Designer Dinesh Kashyap, Conrad Van Dyk

Project Managers Deepali Salvi, Jatin Mehta

Additional Editorial and Design Lydia Baillie, Simon Davis, Sylvia Tombesi-Walton, Conrad Van Dyk

Additional Photography Dorota and Mariusz Jarymowiczowie, Demetrio Carrasco

Picture Credits

t=top; tc–top centre; tr=top right; cla=centre left above; ca=centre above; cra=centre right above; cl=centre left; c=centre; cr=centre right; clb=centre left below; cb=centre below; crb=centre right below; bl=bottom left; bc=bottom centre; br=bottom right.

Every effort has been made to trace the copyright holders, and we apologise in advance for any unintentional omissions. We would be pleased to insert the appropriate acknowledgments in any subsequent edition of this publication.

The Publisher would like to thank the following for their kind assistance and permission to photograph their establishments: 2nd Birkegade, Amalienborg Slot, Bertrams Hotel Guldsmeden, Birger Christensen, Café Ketchup, Café Ultimo, Centralhjørnet, Christiansborg Slot, Christians Kirke, Club Mambo, Copenhagen Admiral Hotel, Copenhagen Jazz House, Copenhagen Zoo, Culture Box, Danmarks Akvarium, Dansk Jødisk Museum, Designer Zoo, Det Nationalhistoriske Museum på Frederiksborg Slot, Hillerød, Emmerys, Experimentarium,

Formel B, Frederiks Kirke (Marmorkirken), Gefährlich, Guinness World Records Museum, Hotel Fox, Illums Bolighus, Jailhouse Event Bar/ Restaurant, Kunstindustrimuseet, La Glace, Louisiana Museum, Magasin du Nord, Masken Bar & Café, Mojo Blues Bar, Museum Erotica, Nasa (club), Nationalmuseet, Ny Carlsberg Glyptotek, Opera House, Orlogsmuseet, Pritzker Price (Keith Walker) for making available the photographs of the interiors of Jørn Utzon's house, Pussy Galore's Flying Circus, Rosenborg Slot, Roskilde Museum, Rundetårn, Sneaky Fox, Søpavillonen, Sofiekælderen, Søstrene Olsen, Tage Anderson, Teatermuseet i Hofteatret, Thé à la Menthe, The Laundromat Café, The Paul, The Square Copenhagen, Tivoli, Vikingeskibsmuseet, Vor Frue Kirke, Zoo Bar.

Works of art have been reproduced with the kind permission of the following copyright holders:
Louise Bourgeois, *Eyes* (1997) © DACS, London/VAGA, New York 101tl; Henry Moore, *Two Piece Reclining Figure No. 5, 1963-64* (LH 517) © The Henry Moore Foundation 101tr.

The publisher would like to thank the following individuals, companies and picture libraries for their kind permissions to reproduce their photographs:

4CORNERS IMAGES:
SIME / Mezzanotte Susy 94–5.

ALAMY: nagelestock.com 72–3.

CORBIS: Archivo Iconografico, S.A. 33tl, 33tr.

DK IMAGES: David Borland 96tr.

FREDERIKSBORG SLOT: Larsen Lennart 32t; Hans Petersen 32br.

INTOXICA BAR -TIKI BAR & KITCHEN: 70tr

JØRN UTZON: 62cr.

OLDR˘ICH KARASEK: 20–21c.

LONELY PLANET IMAGES:
Anders Blomqvist 60–61.

NATIONALMUSEET: 7clb, 26cr, 26br, 27tl, 27bl, 27cra.

NIKOLAJ STEEN MØLLER: 71tl.

ROSENBORG SLOT: 15ca, 74tl.

STATENS MUSEUM FOR KUNST: 22c, 22bc, 23tr, 23c.

SUPERSTOCK:
Brian Lawrence 4–5.

RUST: 81tl

TIVOLI: 10–11c.

VISIT DENMARK: 3bl, 38tc, 10cla; Ireneusz Cyranek 34tr; Danmarks Turistrad 102tl; Bob Krist 34bl; Nicolai Perjesi 34tc; Ukendt 6ca.

All other images © Dorling Kindersley.

For further information see: www.dkimages.com.

Phrase Book

In an Emergency

Help!	**Hjælp!**	yellb!
Stop!	**Stands!**	stanns!
Can you call a doctor?	**Kan du tilkalde en læge?**	kann do till-kalleh ehn laiyeh?
Can you call an ambulance?	**Kan du tilkalde en ambulance?**	kann do till-kalleh ehn ahm-boo-lang-seh?
Can you call the police?	**Kan du tilkalde politiet?**	kann do till-kalleh po-ly-tee'd?
Can you call the fire brigade?	**Kan du tilkalde brand-væsenet?**	kann do till-kalleh brahn-vaiys-ned?
Is there a telephone here?	**Er der en telefon i nærheden?**	e-ah dah ehn tele-fohn ee neya-hethen?
Where is the nearest hospital?	**Hvor er det nærmeste hospital?**	voa e-ah deh neh-meste hoh-spee-tahl

Useful Phrases

Sorry	**Undskyld**	ons-gull
Goodnight	**Godnat**	goh-nad
Goodbye	**Farvel**	fah-vell
Good evening	**Godaften**	goh-ahf-tehn
Good morning	**Godmorgen**	goh-moh'n
Good morning (after about 9am)	**Goddag**	goh-dah
Yes	**Ja**	yah
No	**Nej**	nye
Please	**Værsgo/ Velbekomme**	vehs-goh/ vell-beh-commeh
Thank you	**Tak**	tahgg
How are you?	**Hvordan har du det?/ Hvordan går det?**	voh-dann hah do deh?/ voh-dan go deh?
Well, thank you	**Godt, tak**	gohd, tahgg
Pleased to have met you	**Det var rart at møde dig**	deh vah rahd add meutheh die
See you!	**Vi ses!**	vee sehs!
I understand	**Jeg forstår**	yay fuh-stoah
I don't understand	**Jeg forstår ikke**	yay fuh-stoah egge
Does anyone speak English?	**Er der nogen, der kan tale engelsk?**	e-ah dah noh-enn dah kann tah-leh eng-ellsgg?
good	**god**	guth
bad	**dårlig**	doh-lee
up	**op**	ohb
down	**ned**	neth
near	**tæt på**	taid poh
far	**langt fra**	lahngd fra
on the left	**til venstre**	till vehn-streh
on the right	**til højre**	till hoy-reh
open	**åben**	oh-ben
closed	**lukket**	luh-geth
warm	**varm**	vahm
cold	**kold**	koll
big	**stor**	stoah
little	**lille**	lee-leh

Making a Telephone Call

Whom am I speaking to?	**Hvem taler jeg med?**	vemm talah yay meth?
I would like to call...	**Jeg vil gerne ringe til...**	yay vill geh-neh ring-eh till...
I will telephone again	**Jeg ringer en gang til**	yay ring-ah ehn gahng till

In a Hotel

Do you have double rooms?	**Findes her dobbelt-værelser?**	feh-ness he-ah dob-belld vah-hel-sah?
With bathroom	**Med bade-værelse**	meth bah-the-vah-hel-sah
With washbasin	**Med hånd-vask**	meth hohn-vasgg
key	**nøgle**	noy-leh
I have a reservation	**Jeg har en reservation**	yay hah ehn res-sah-vah-shohn

Sightseeing

entrance	**indgang**	ehn-gahng
exit	**udgang**	ooth-gahng
exhibition	**udstilling**	ooth-stelling
tourist information	**turisto-plysning**	tooh-reesd-ohb-lehs-ning
town/city hall	**rådhus**	rahd-hus
post office	**posthus**	posd-hus
cathedral	**domkirke**	dom-kia-keh
church	**kirke**	kia-keh
museum	**museum**	muh-seh-uhm
town bus	**bybus**	bih-boos
long-distance bus	**rutebil**	roo-teh-beel
railway station	**banegård**	bah-neh-goh
airport	**lufthavn**	luhft-havn
train	**tog**	toh
ferry terminal	**færgehavn**	fah-veh-havn
bus stop	**busstoppested**	buhs-sdob-beh-steth
long-distance bus station	**rutebilstation**	roo-teh-beel-sta-shion
a public toilet	**et offentligt toilet**	ehd off-end-ligd toa-led

Shopping

I wish to buy...	**Jeg vil gerne købe...**	yay vill geh-neh kyh-beh...
Do you have...?	**Findes der...?**	feh-ness de-ah...?
How much does it cost?	**Hvad koster det?**	vath koh-stah deh
expensive	**dyr**	dyh-ah
cheap	**billig**	billy
size	**størrelse**	stoh-ell-seh
general store	**købmand**	keuhb-mann
greengrocer	**grønthandler**	grund-handla
supermarket	**supermarked**	suh-pah-mah-keth
market	**marked**	mah-keth

Eating Out

Do you have a table for... people?	**Har I et bord til... personer?**	hah ee ed boah till... peh-soh-nah?
I would like to	**Jeg vil gerne**	yay vill geh-neh

sit by the window	**sidde ved vinduet**	saithe veth veen-do-ed
I wish to order...	**Jeg vil gerne bestille...**	yay vill geh-neh beh-stilleh...
I'm a vegetarian	**Jeg er vegetar**	yay eh-ah veh-gehta
children's menu	**børnemenu**	byeh-neh-meh-nye
daily special	**dagens ret**	dayens rad
starter	**forret**	foh-red
main course	**hovedret**	hoh-veth-red
dessert	**dessert**	deh-seh'd
wine list	**vinkort**	veen-cod
sweet	**sødt**	sodt
sour	**surt**	suad
spicy	**stærkt**	stehgd
May I have the bill?	**Må jeg bede om regningen?**	moh yay beh-theh uhm rahy-ning-ehn

Menu Decoder

agurk	**cucumber**	a-guag
ananas	**pineapple**	a-nah-nas
appelsin	**orange**	abbel-seen
blomme	**plum**	blum-ma
brød	**bread**	bruth
champignon	**mushroom**	sham-pee-ong
danskvand	**mineral water**	dansg vann
fersken	**peach**	fes-gehn
fisk	**fish**	fesgg
fløde	**cream**	flu-theh
gulerod	**carrot**	gooleh-roth
grøntsager	**vegetables**	grunn-saha
hummer	**lobster**	humma
is	**ice cream**	ees
kaffe	**coffee**	kah-feh
kartofler	**potatoes**	kah-toff-lah
kød	**meat**	kuth
kylling	**chicken**	killing
kål	**cabbage**	kohl
laks	**salmon**	lahggs
lam	**lamb**	lahm
leverpostej	**liver paté**	leh-vah-poh-stie
løg	**onion**	loy
mælk	**milk**	mailgg
oksekød	**beef**	ogg-seh-kuth
ost	**cheese**	ossd
peber	**pepper**	peh-ba
pore	**leek**	po-a
purløj	**chives**	poo-a-loy
pølse	**sausage**	pill-seh
rejer	**shrimps**	rah-yah
ris	**rice**	rees
rødspætte	**plaice**	roth-speh-da
røget fisk	**smoked fish**	roy-heth fesgg
saftevand	**squash**	sah-fteh-vann
salat	**salad**	sah-lad
salt	**salt**	sald
sild	**herring**	sil
skaldyr	**shellfish**	sgall-dya
skinke	**ham**	sgeng-geh
smør	**butter**	smuah
sodavand	**fizzy drink**	sodah-vann
steg	**steak**	stie
svinekød	**pork**	svee-neh-kuth
syltetøj	**jam**	sill-teh-toi
te	**tea**	teh
tærte	**quiche/pie**	te-ah-teh

torsk	**cod**	tohsgg
vand	**water**	vann
wienerbrød	**Danish pastry**	vee-nah-bryd
æble	**apple**	eh-bleh
æg	**egg**	egg
øl	**beer**	uhl

Time

today	**i dag**	ee-day
tomorrow	**i morgen**	ee-mohn
yesterday	**i går**	ee-goh
before noon	**formiddag**	foh-medday
afternoon	**eftermiddag**	ehftah-medday
evening	**aften**	ahftehn
night	**nat**	nadd
minute	**minut**	meh-nude
hour	**time**	tee-meh
week	**uge**	oo-eh
month	**måned**	moe-neth
year	**år**	oah

Days of the Week

Monday	**mandag**	mann-day
Tuesday	**tirsdag**	teahs-day
Wednesday	**onsdag**	uns-day
Thursday	**torsdag**	toahs-day
Friday	**fredag**	frey-day
Saturday	**lørdag**	lur-day
Sunday	**søndag**	son-day

Months

January	**januar**	ya-nuah
February	**februar**	fib-buah
March	**marts**	mahds
April	**april**	apreal
May	**maj**	mai
June	**juni**	yoo-nee
July	**juli**	yoo-lee
August	**august**	auw-guhsd
September	**september**	sehb-tem-bah
October	**oktober**	ogg-toh-bah
November	**november**	noh-vem-bah
December	**december**	deh-sem-bah

Numbers

0	**nul**	noll
1	**en**	ehn
2	**to**	toh
3	**tre**	tray
4	**fire**	fee-ah
5	**fem**	femm
6	**seks**	seggs
7	**syv**	siu
8	**otte**	oh-deh
9	**ni**	nee
10	**ti**	tee
20	**tyve**	tyh-veh
30	**tredive**	traith-veh
40	**fyrre**	fyr-reh
50	**halvtreds**	hahl-traiths
60	**tres**	traiths
70	**halvfjerds**	hahl-fyads
80	**firs**	fee-ahs
90	**halvfems**	hahl-femms
100	**hundrede**	hoon-dreh-the
200	**tohundrede**	toh-hoon-dreh-the
1,000	**tusind**	tooh-sin-deh
2,000	**totusinde**	toh-tooh-sin-deh

Selected Street Index